TRUE LOVE

JENNIFER LOPEZ

PHOTOS BY ANA CARBALLOSA

CELEBRA
Published by New American Library,
an imprint of Penguin Random House LLC
375 Hudson Street, New York, New York 10014

This book is a publication of New American Library. Previously published in a Celebra
hardcover edition.

First Celebra Trade Paperback Printing, November 2015

For more information about Penguin Random House, visit penguin.com.

CELEBRA TRADE PAPERBACK ISBN 978-0-451-46869-7

THE LIBRARY OF CONGRESS HAS CATALOGED THE HARDCOVER EDITION OF THIS TITLE AS FOLLOWS:
Lopez, Jennifer, 1970–
True love/by Jennifer Lopez.
p. cm.
ISBN 978-0-451-46868-0
1. Lopez, Jennifer, 1970– 2. Motion picture actors and actresses—United States—Biography.
3. Singers—United States—Biography. I. Title.
PN2287.L634A3 2013
791.4302'8092--dc23   2013027047
[B]

Printed in the United States of America
10 9 8 7 6 5 4 3 2 1

Set in Bembo Std
Designed by Pauline Neuwirth

PUBLISHER'S NOTE
Penguin is committed to publishing works of quality and integrity. In that spirit, we are proud
to offer this book to our readers; however the story, the experiences and the words are the
author's alone.

Owning our story can be hard but not nearly as difficult as spending our lives running from it. Embracing our vulnerabilities is risky but not nearly as dangerous as giving up on love and belonging and joy—the experiences that make us the most vulnerable. Only when we are brave enough to explore the darkness will we discover the infinite power of our light.

—Brené Brown, *The Gifts of Imperfection*

This book is dedicated to Max and Emme,
who saved me.

CONTENTS

PREFACE

IT'S OPENING NIGHT, the first show of my first ever world tour.

This was the first time we'd be doing the full show that we had been planning and working on for more than six months. I am in full costume, backstage with the usual cast of characters. I bend down to give Emme and Max a kiss before my mom walks them off to watch the opening of the show. This was going to be the first time they'd see their mommy perform in front of thousands and thousands of people. The last time I was on stage like this, they were in my belly.

As they walk away, Emme looks back and stops. I'm being buckled into the rig on a twelve-by-twelve-inch platform. The huge, full-feather train of my white skirt pours over the edges and it must seem to her like I'm standing in a cloud. She seems a little nervous, but excited. I'm nervous, but controlling my fear. I'm about to ascend sixty feet into the air. I know it's crazy, because the crew is watching with faces that say, *This is crazy!* I give the operator the thumbs-up; he gives me the thumbs-up in return . . . and up I go, disappearing into the rafters until I am perched behind a huge video wall, where nobody can see me.

Emme looks up, watching me rise and rise and rise . . . From my perspective, everybody looks like little ants on the floor. I take a deep breath and think about the past year, all the hard work and the hard lessons that have led to this moment.

If I let myself, I could go weak in the knees. But I don't. I hold strong as the band plays the dramatic intro while the opening movie plays on the screen. And when the video wall splits open, I'm standing there, a hundred feet above the audience, and the crowd goes wild. The spotlight hits me, and in my best old Hollywood voice I say: "HELLO, LOVERS."

In this book I'm going to take you on the physical and emotional journey of the year I went on the first world tour of my career. The year that changed my life.

When I started planning the tour, I knew it was going to be the anchor for a very personal show. What I didn't expect was how cathartic it would end up being for me. The process of building the tour and performing it each and every night for audiences around the world helped me get back to who I am—someone who sings, who dances, who expresses herself and connects with people through music.

So many times I wanted to abandon writing this book because I knew it would be a difficult process, delving into the past and reliving some of my darkest moments. Also, I didn't want to be misread. I didn't want anything to overshadow the magnificence of this great journey. This book is not a detailed account of any of my relationships, famous or not. This is not a "tell-all," so I hope that's not what you're looking for. But by the end, I think you'll agree, you'll have gotten so much more. This book is about a series of patterns that go back as early as my childhood. This book is about *my* path and what *I* learned. It's the story of

a transformative journey where I faced some of my greatest challenges, overcame some of my biggest fears, and emerged a stronger person than I've ever been. This is the story of how I discovered . . . the truest love of all.

My genuine intention and what I hope to accomplish with this book is that others can draw upon the experiences that changed the course of my life and find encouragement in the mantra that motivated the following pages:

You will live.

You will love.

You will *dance again* . . .

SETTING THE STAGE

I wake up in bed alone. The silence in my room reminds me of the emptiness in my heart. I failed at love—again. Except this time, it wasn't just me. I am haunted by the inescapable thought that I let down my beautiful babies, Max and Emme. I wanted so badly for things to have turned out differently.

As lonely as this bed feels, I can't bring myself to get out of it.

ROCK BOTTOM

HITTING ROCK BOTTOM

I remember the exact moment when everything changed. I was in the desert outside Los Angeles, getting ready for a photo shoot.

It was a beautiful day in July 2011, and Marc and I had just celebrated our seventh wedding anniversary. Anybody looking from the outside in would have thought my life was going great: I had a husband and two beautiful children, and my career was flying high. I was on *American Idol*, the number-one show on the planet, and my new single "On the Floor" had gone to number one all over the world. To top it off, *People* magazine had named me their very first Most Beautiful Woman in the World, a few months earlier. How could life get any better?

What people didn't know was that life really *wasn't* that good. My relationship was falling apart, and I was terrified.

And now here I was out in the desert, getting made up for a L'Oréal shoot. I had done hundreds of these before—you sit in the chair, get your hair and face made up, go out in front of the camera, and do your thing. But this day didn't feel like any other day.

As I sat there, my mind was racing. My heart was beating out of my chest, and I felt like I couldn't breathe . . . I became consumed with fear and anxiety. *What was happening to me?*

My mom, Guadalupe, who lives in New York and happened to be in town that week, came to the desert with me that day, and my dear manager, Benny Medina, was there too. As I found myself in a panic, I leaped from my chair and said, "Benny, something is happening! I feel like I'm going crazy."

In the end, the truth finds a way to surface, even if you don't want it to.

Benny, who has been through so much with me over the fifteen years we have worked together and been friends, took my hands.

"Hey, now, what's happening? What's going on?" he asked.

My mom rushed to my side, too, a look of concern on her face.

All I could say was, "I don't know. I don't feel right. I'm scared. I feel like I'm losing my mind."

He tried to calm me down, saying, "You're fine, Jennifer. You're good. Everything's okay." To him I looked completely calm. But I wasn't. It was one of those moments when you're so scared you can't even scream. It feels as if you're paralyzed.

We as human beings do this thing where we stuff down our feelings until they find a way to manifest themselves. We try to avoid them until there's no more room and they come bubbling up like a pot of boiling-hot water that overflows. And when it does, it burns, and it's scary. That's what was happening to me.

In a blur of fear and panic, I looked at Benny and my mother and blurted out the words: "I don't think I can be with Marc anymore." Then I burst into tears.

It was out.

The one thing I feared more than anything in the world. The one thing I had been trying for so long not to face. Deep down, I knew that nothing would ever be the same again.

I collapsed into their arms and began to sob. And like that pot of boiling-hot water, once it overflows, the pressure is released and it begins to cool down. All those crazy thoughts started to melt away because I had finally given voice to the real reason for my fear and panic. I knew what it meant to say those words out loud: It meant the end of my marriage. The end of our family. The end of the dream I had worked so hard to hold together.

And it meant more than that. It meant that once again I was going to be judged. I was going to be ridiculed, chastised, and mocked. I could already see the headlines: "Jennifer Lopez Headed for Divorce . . . Again!" Or, "The Woman Who Has Everything But Can't Get Love Right!" I was so scared to have another failure, to be scrutinized by the world, and to disappoint everyone . . . again.

But this time wasn't like any other time. It was worse. This divorce wouldn't affect just Marc and me. It would affect these two beautiful little souls we had brought into the world. I was devastated at the thought of hurting Max and Emme. I was afraid that I was about to ruin their lives, that someday they would resent me for not being able to keep this marriage together.

As I struggled with the idea of breaking up my family, I had to consider what was best for my kids in the long run, and I agonized over what would serve them best in life. I was pulled in both directions, which is why I had fought so hard against admitting the inevitable. I *couldn't* admit that this marriage was over. But in the end, the truth finds a way to surface, even if you don't want it to. That day in the desert, with my brain going wild trying to deny reality, I had finally hit rock bottom.

HOPE FOR A BETTER DAY

On Christmas day in 2010, seven months before that L'Oréal photo shoot, we had a house full of people. Marc was there, and Emme and Max, and Marc's other kids, Ryan and Cristian, Arianna and Alex, as well as our parents, siblings, and friends. It was the kind of Christmas gathering I'd always wanted to have: a big, sprawling affair with our family at the center of it.

The house was filled with food and gifts and laughter, and that afternoon, twenty-four of us sat down to a beautiful Christmas dinner. Things between Marc and me weren't perfect, of course—our marriage was never the kind to glide along peacefully. From the beginning, it was tumultuous, passionate, and explosive, but we also shared many fulfilling and joyful moments. I knew we had problems, but we loved each other and we were trying, and I wanted more than anything to have a family—*this* family. So I was willing to ignore whatever wasn't going well, for the greater good of preserving it.

I thought that Christmas was exactly what I wanted. I thought we were finally getting it right, that it was worth putting up with the difficulties because this was what life was about. Every marriage has its challenges, but it was about keeping that marriage together, having that family unit, and making the dream come true—whatever the cost. Part of that concept still holds true for me: Family is most important.

But the very next Christmas, twelve months later, I was waking up alone. The only people in the house were Max, Emme, and my cousin Tiana, who had come to keep me company. My mother and my sisters, Lynda and Leslie, had decided to stay in New York for the holidays, and they had asked me to come out, but I didn't want to go. I wanted to be in my own home, as empty as it now felt.

I cried a lot that Christmas, though I tried to let the tears flow only when the kids couldn't see me. There's nothing like the holidays to make you feel a loss, and I was really feeling it. But then my dad, David, came over for Christmas dinner, and Benny came and brought his mom. So with Emme, Max, and everyone else, we had a pretty full table—even if it wasn't as full as the one we had the year before.

What I will always remember about that Christmas is not the tears or the loneliness, but the toast that Benny gave.

Benny Medina is a legend in his own right. He's the original inspiration for the Fresh Prince of Bel-Air—a larger-than-life guy who always manages to make everyone around him feel special. He's also famous among his friends for his "Benny toasts." He loves to seize the moment, to raise his glass and offer up a story, a speech, or an affirmation. He works on them—you can sometimes see him typing out words on his phone right before he gets up to speak. So when Benny raises his glass, you know you're about to hear something special. And that dinner was no exception.

"A lot of changes have happened over this past year," he said. "There has been loss, and there has been gain. Look around you and remember that this family—the family that is sitting here with you—has always been here. And we will always be here."

I looked around the table at all these people I loved: my dad, my babies, Tiana, my cousins, my aunt, Benny.

"You make your choices in life, and these people right here," he said, "these people are the family that will get you through. They are your rock."

"You make your choices in life, and these people right here," he said, "these people are the family that will get you through. They are your rock."

As he spoke, I began to see that I did have people around me who supported and loved me unconditionally and had always been there. Families come in all shapes and sizes, and they don't have to fit the perfect dream ideal to make you happy. They are the people that support and love you by giving you strength when you need it the most.

As I looked around the table, it hit me; he was right. I felt the love. I felt that family. And I knew I was blessed.

I hoped that he was right about something else too. He said, "As painful as some of the past year's changes have been, they will ultimately lead to a better place. The adversity you come across in life may cause pain, but with pain comes growth and the opportunity to rise to the occasion as your strongest, best self."

There was nothing I needed more in that moment than the encouragement and the hope of a better day.

Benny's speech gave me that beautiful gift.

NEW DREAM

In my family, when I was growing up, divorce was not an option. My parents stayed together for thirty-three years, through thick and thin and everything in between. So when I married Marc, having already been through the disappointment of two divorces and a broken engagement, I wanted so much for our marriage to be "it." I was determined to make it last, no matter what. And once we had kids, I was even more determined. I was never going to give up on this love.

Tried to be someone I knew that I wasn't
I thought I could make myself happy with you

—"NEVER GONNA GIVE UP"

Marc was my guy, the one. The father of my children, the man I was going to grow old with. I believed that with all my heart . . . until I finally realized, in the months leading up to that day in the desert, that it wasn't meant to be. I wasn't listening to my own inner voice, and now my body and soul were physically telling me that I could no longer be there. I couldn't deny the truth anymore. I had to do something about it.

When I think back on it, years earlier I had reached a similar moment in my career. It was during a time when I was getting to do things that I had hardly let myself dream about when I was a little girl. Platinum albums, movie roles opposite Jack Nicholson, George Clooney, Sean Penn . . . I felt like I was doing it on my own terms, but actually, I wasn't.

I was mainly following the advice of managers, record executives, and stylists. They had the best of intentions, but because I wasn't also listening to myself, I ended up caring more and more about what they wanted and how I was perceived by the public and the media than what I knew was right for me as an artist. Instead of measuring my success and value by my own standards, I was measuring it by how others perceived me.

Because I was so used to being seen as that woman in the tabloids, the Hollywood diva, I forgot what it was like to be known as myself. It's vital to be in touch with who you are at your core and not to lose yourself in the hustle. I had always wanted to believe that my public image didn't affect my feelings of self-worth—but unfortunately, that wasn't always the case. If you keep hearing negative things about yourself, they start to seep into your consciousness and you start to feel like they're true. They cloud who you know you really are and you can lose yourself.

I was being painted in a way that wasn't me because I wasn't taking control of the situation. I was so wrapped up in keeping up with my schedule and giving people what they wanted that I neglected to ask myself what *I* wanted. I spent a lot of energy living up to those expectations and I lost my own sense of direction along the way.

When I first started my career, I always made my decisions on my own; I always knew what was best for me. I didn't have anyone telling me what to do or where to go. I followed my heart, followed my instincts, and listened to my gut. Because the truth is, nobody knows what's best for you better than you do. You have to really sit still and ask yourself: *What do I want? Does this feel right? What should I do?* I realized I had to go back and do what I had always done. Listening to my gut was just as important as listening to the advice of others, and only I knew what was best for me.

That's why now, whenever someone asks me, "What is the one piece of advice you would give an artist who is starting out and wants to do what you do?"

My answer is always: "Listen to yourself; listen to your gut. Because only you know what's right for you."

That's what being an artist is all about. Your power is in your individuality, in being exactly who you are. No two artists are alike, just like no two people are alike. That's why there is no competition in artistry. It's not about being the best or the biggest, the king or the queen. That notion is so ridiculous. That competition or comparison is actually the exact opposite of what being an artist is. As an artist, you should be in competition with only one person—yourself. You can't worry about what others are doing or saying. You have to keep that focus and stay true to who you are in order to be creative and make the best decisions.

As an artist, you should be in competition with only one person—yourself.

So when I came to a point where my relationship simply wasn't feeling right, I knew what I needed to do. If I turned down the noise from the rest of the world—critics, fans, friends, even family—and if I really listened to myself, what would I hear?

I had to ask myself that question. So just like I took control of my career in that crucial moment, now I needed to take control of my life.

"You make your choices in life," Benny had said in his toast. Now that my marriage was over and my life was going in a different direction than I'd thought, I had another choice to make, and this time I was determined to make it for myself. I began to ask: *What's next? What new dream am I going to build now?* In the days following that Christmas dinner, this was the question I kept coming back to. I simply couldn't ignore it.

CONQUERING THE WORLD

By January first, I had faced my worst fear: the breakup of our seemingly perfect family. Reality was setting in, and I needed to figure out how to make it all work. I was a single mom now: *How am I going to do this? Can I do this? Can I be their everything? Will I ever be able to fill that hole for them?*

Can just Mommy ever be enough? It was daunting and, at times, depressing to realize that I didn't always have the answers. It was even scarier to think that maybe I never would. But I couldn't stop to think about that now. I had to see it through. Even in my weakest moments, the moments when I doubted myself the most, my babies needed me. I had to be strong.

I don't know what it is about me, but for better or for worse, in the face of doubt or change, I get these crazy ideas—don't ask me why—that I should challenge myself beyond my normal limits and do something I've never done before. I guess, subconsciously, it's about distracting myself from the difficulty and pain of the moment. Example: After I had the kids—talk about a big change—I really felt like I'd lost my mojo. I was exhausted, out of shape, and I felt like a beached whale. So what did I do? I decided to do a triathlon! Now, understand, I had never done a triathlon before. I had run a 10K when I was twelve, but never anything close to a triathlon.

On the morning of the race, as I was standing there surrounded by a thousand paparazzi, about to jump into the ocean, I realized that this probably wasn't the best idea I ever had. All I could see was a buoy five hundred meters out, and the only thing blocking its view were the waves crashing toward me. The one prayer I kept saying over and over again was: "Please, God, I have two babies. Please let me survive this incredibly stupid thing I decided to do." But when the gun went off, I instinctually ran toward the ocean and jumped in. I faced my fear, and when I crossed that finish line, I felt invincible. I'd gotten my mojo back. I felt like I could do anything.

Now it was happening again. After a reflective Christmas and a New Year's I'd been trying to make the best of, it was one in the afternoon and I was lying in bed all by myself, staring at the ceiling. And then it hit me. One of those crazy ideas popped into my head. I picked up the phone to call Benny. The conversation went a little like this:

"Benny! I know what I want to do," I said.

"Yeah?" he responded.

And in a quiet, determined tone that Benny has come to know means I've had a revelation, I said: "I *have* to tour this year. That's what we have to do."

"Really?" said Benny. He paused for a moment. Benny had wanted

this for years. I awaited his response: "Okay . . . Let's do it," he finally said.

"Okay, then!" I said. "Let's do it."

"Okay cool . . ."

"Great! I'm excited," I said.

"I'm excited too," he said.

I hung up. End call.

What the hell had I done? Oh. My. God. What now?

PAAAAANIIIIIICCCCC!!!!

See? It was working! I was no longer focused on my sadness; my thoughts were somewhere else, on the colossal challenge I had put on myself of building my "new dream." Something that would take me through five continents, sixty-five cities, four hundred and sixty-two wardrobe changes, and five hundred thousand sequins (*I hoped*): my first ever world tour.

Despite what many people might think, I had never done a tour before. And, on top of it all, I was about to do it as a single mom, with two kids in tow.

ACT ONE

BIG HOLLYWOOD

SET LIST

Intro: "Never Gonna Give Up"

———

"Get Right"

———

"Love Don't Cost a Thing"

———

"I'm Into You"

———

"Waiting for Tonight"

———

I was sad. I was heartbroken. I was scared.

But it was only through adversity that I found

my saving graces.

Sometimes they came from unexpected

sources—a song, a challenge, or a friend.

It was my responsibility to make the most of

them, apply them to my life, act on them, and

rise to the occasion.

NEVER GONNA GIVE UP

BECAUSE I HAD never done a solo tour before, I wanted to get it just right. I wanted to tell a story, to open myself up to people, to give them what they'd been waiting to see. I made my first record back in 1999, which meant that some people had been waiting thirteen years for me to come and do a show. I wanted to do all the hits for them; I wanted them to feel it had been worth the wait.

If I was going to do this, I'd have to work incredibly hard, and my goal was not only to grow as an artist, but also as a person. A part of me was petrified to take it on, as I knew there was a possibility that it might not turn out right. Yet part of me was so drawn by the fantasy of it. *What would I do creatively if I could do anything at all? What songs would I choose? How would I express myself as an artist?* And more important: *What was I going to wear? Who would make my costumes?* This could actually be a lot of fun! In designing the tour, I suddenly had this empty canvas that I could paint however I liked. But as with any blank canvas, facing it was both exciting and daunting. *Where do I begin? What do I want to say? What is my message?* I needed a concept to start with.

THE GIFT OF SONG

Right before my breakup, Enrique Iglesias called to say he wanted to do a duet with me. He sent me a song and we recorded it, but after he listened to it, he told me, "It's not a big enough hit. If you and I do a song together, it has to be a smash. I'm sending you another song."

He sent me a song called "Dance Again." By then, a couple of months had gone by and Marc and I had just split up. I was dying inside, feeling lonely and miserable and sad. I don't remember the song's exact original lyrics, but it had the chorus, "I want to dance . . . and love . . . and *dance again*." All I could think was, "Oh my God, that's what I want. I want to *dance and love and dance again* too."

I needed that song. I was at a moment in my life where I felt like I might not be happy ever again. That line expressed everything I was feeling.

I'm a dancer—that's who I am. I'm most happy and free and alive when I'm dancing. I wanted to get back to that feeling, that person. I wanted to feel happiness again. I wanted to feel love again. And that's what music does. Music is a declaration of what life is and what you want it to be.

And the sentiment of that song . . . was something I wanted to declare to the world.

This was *my* song.

Oops—record scratch.

Except it wasn't my song. It was Enrique's.

I said to Benny, "Enrique wants to do this as a duet, but I think it would work better if I did it alone. I can't just ask him to let me have it for my record, right?"

Benny said, "Well, *I* can. Let me talk to him." I don't know exactly what he said, but in the end, Enrique gave me the song.

As fate would have it, Enrique and I wound up doing the US leg of the tour together. I'll never forget opening night in New York. Enrique came up to me at the end of the show, after seeing people's response to "Dance Again." He looked me in the eyes and said, "Jennifer, you were right. That really *is* your song."

When Enrique gave me that song, he gave me a powerful gift. In some ways, every song is like that, because music is a gift in itself. When you listen to the right tune, and the lyrics express your soul's truest feelings, it lifts you up—it's a beautiful thing. I'd felt it as a young girl, listening to songs on the radio. And now, as an artist, to be able to make that music and sing it—sing it for myself, sing it for others—is one of my biggest blessings from God.

When you listen to the right tune, and the lyrics express your soul's truest feelings, it lifts you up—it's a beautiful thing.

I remember Puffy once saying to me while I was making my very first album, "Be careful what you sing, be careful what you record because it can define you." Music is very powerful. It goes out into the universe, and it takes on an energy; it becomes part of your story. That's why I would never record anything that's too negative or too depressing—because that's not what I want my life to be about. Music isn't just songs, it's your life as an artist. In many ways, you sing your future. I believed that and it always rang true with me. At this moment in my life, on a very visceral level, I wanted to dance again and I wanted to love again so I wanted to sing about it. I feel like every song I've recorded has been given to me in some way—every song has come to me at the right moment. And now, with Enrique's gift, I felt that way again.

Once I had the song, everything flowed from there. We named the new greatest hits record *Dance Again*, and when we released the single, it made it to the top ten in countries all over the world. Everything became about that message.

The Dance Again World Tour was born.

I wanted to *dance again* . . . and for the first time, I was about to do it all over the world.

JUMPING IN

The truth was, I had planned to do a world tour three or four times in the past. We'd do all the planning and get all the way to the stage where we were making the deals—and then I'd get a part in a movie. A tour you can move around, but when a movie comes up, it shoots when it shoots, and you're either in or you're out. So we would always say, "Okay, let's move the tour dates." And then somehow, even though we meant only to postpone, it always ended up falling apart. But because my records kept selling, even without the tours to support them, nobody seemed to mind that they weren't happening.

Many people seemed to doubt I could actually *do* a tour. Never having done one, I have to admit, I wasn't sure either. Would I have the stamina to be on the road so long? Could I really sing live and dance and do all those shows all those nights in a row? Would my voice hold up? Would it be too much for the kids?

Over the following weeks, I'd call Benny and say, "Listen, forget what I said. This isn't the right time." He'd try to calm me, and sometimes it worked and sometimes it didn't. We went back and forth, talking and thinking and weighing it all out. The tour was on; the tour was off. In my heart I knew I could do it, but my brain kept pulling me back.

As I considered the reality of doing this tour, I remembered a peculiar thing that had happened a decade earlier, when I was in Canada shooting the movie *Angel Eyes*. Everybody on set kept talking about this amazing psychic who lived in Toronto. I don't usually go for that kind of thing, but people kept saying how incredible this guy was. "You have to go see him! He'll read you like a book!" I was young and having fun, and so a couple of us decided, for the hell of it, to jump in the car and go see him.

I went with a girlfriend I've known since elementary school and who was working for me at the time. We found the psychic's place, and when I'd settled in for my reading, he looked at me and got very serious.

"Whenever you end up going on tour," he said, "it's going to be more than traveling around and doing shows. You're going to grow as a person."

This seemed like a strange thing for a psychic to latch onto, but then the guy actually started to get kind of emotional.

"I'm telling you," he said, "going on tour will change your life. It will change everything about you."

I looked at him and was shocked to see that he had tears in his eyes. It was so intense, so unexpected. So *weird*. And he wasn't finished.

"Spiritually," he said, "as a human being, it will take you to the next level."

Now, I don't know that I really believed in all of what he had to say, but I never forgot his words. And as I was going back and forth with Benny—I have to be honest—I found myself thinking about it. "Maybe if we do this, something really amazing *will* happen!" And after all the pain I'd been through, I wanted my old self back—strong me, happy me, dancing me. Maybe this tour was the answer.

So finally, when the clock had ticked down to our do-or-die moment, Benny stopped me and said, "They need to know right now, kiddo."

I was standing in my trailer about to go on live TV for *Idol*. I took a step back, took a deep breath, and said, "I'll do it."

A month later, we were in rehearsals.

Figuring it out what this is all about
when he came to me, when he comes to me
Gotta do what's best for me

—"NEVER GONNA GIVE UP"

I wanted the show to start like a scene out of an old Hollywood musical. I didn't want it to feel real; I wanted it to feel like a movie, like

people were watching the Ziegfeld Follies, with Rita Hayworth, or Ava Gardner, gliding across the stage.

On the walls of the den in my house, I have black-and-white photos of Hollywood stars from the thirties, forties, and fifties. When you look at those photos, you can imagine yourself right there with them, in a scene out of a classic movie. And I had. So that's how I wanted the opening of the show to feel. Something soft, beautiful, ethereal . . . something magical from another era.

I saw myself sitting at a desk, backstage in my dressing room, writing in a diary, dressed in a white gown, playing the role of the Hollywood star surrounded by dancing men in tuxedos and top hats. I wanted to make them feel like they were watching a dream . . .

As I was imagining this whole scene, I wondered what song I should be singing for it. I knew that "Dance Again" would be the final song, the get-on-your-feet encore, the final message I wanted everyone to

take away from this show. But the first song is just as important, as it sets the stage for everything to come. *What should it be? What do I want this show to be about?* I turned to the person who had become my friend, my partner and collaborator for this show—Beau.

A FRESH PERSPECTIVE

I met Beau about a year earlier when I was doing the video shoot for "On the Floor." While we were in the editing process, I was watching clips with the choreographer, Frank Gatson, when I noticed one of the background dancers doing a really cool move.

"Wait," I said. "That's amazing. Let's put that in. Who is that?"

"That's Casper," said Frank, which is Beau's nickname. At the time, we had just lost one of our dancers and needed a replacement for an upcoming performance. So I said, "Let's bring that guy in. Let's hire him for the show."

Beau was pretty young at the time, but he had done choreography for Eminem and Beyoncé, had worked with artists like Michael Jackson and Pink, and had been on TV shows like *Jimmy Kimmel Live* and *Glee*.

Because I started as a dancer, I have always related to them. I get them, and they get me, and whenever I'm shooting a video or doing a show, I like hanging around them. It's a world I love and feel comfortable in. So right away, I felt a kinship with Beau. He and the other dancers saw me as strong and capable and determined, and slowly, I was able to be strong and capable and determined. In the same way negative influences can bring you down, having positive people around can help lift you up.

We started as creative partners, but eventually we became good friends, truly valuing each other's opinions. So at the time, he was the natural choice to help me put the tour together.

We had already decided that we wanted to do a fifties musical-esque opening that felt dreamy and ethereal, with angelic voices singing some beautiful ballad. So we sat down and went through all the different songs from my albums, trying to figure out which one would intro the show.

"Maybe 'Secretly'?" I said, flipping through pages, looking at lyrics.

In the same way negative influences can bring you down, having positive people around can help lift you up.

"No," Beau said. "It has to be 'Never Gonna Give Up.' It's a perfect statement for you. Because that's who you are." He cued the song up, and we listened:

Now that I'm growing / Now that I'm knowing
Never gonna give up on / Never gonna give up on love . . .

"You're not about to give up on love, right?" he said. "People need to know that. Even though you went through this bad period, that's still how you feel."

He was right. So that's how we opened the show, with that sentiment. Yes, this big thing in my life went wrong, but I'm not gonna give up. I'm never giving up on love.

In the video that intro'd the show, I'm backstage in my flowing white dress, writing about love in my diary, singing about never giving up, about moving to that next chapter in life. *I don't want to hear no woulda coulda, maybe I shoulda . . . Never gonna give up on, never gonna give up on . . . loove looove loooove . . .*

And as the word "love" hangs in the air, I close my book, get up from my desk, and walk through the backstage of an old majestic theater . . . I fearlessly ascend a beautiful white staircase, and step by step, I begin my new journey.

Little did I know this tour would end up helping me reflect on the journey of my life, through my music, in a way that opened my eyes. I never expected it. I never thought, when we first started designing the show, that it would be such a life-changing experience.

When I reach the top of the stairs, the kabuki curtain drops on the real stage, revealing the first act of the show: Big Hollywood.

All of my dreams were coming true. Except for one.

Love proved elusive. But I kept trying. If I could make so many of my dreams come true, why not this?

BIG HOLLYWOOD

ART IMITATING LIFE

And here she is: the Jennifer Lopez that people have been waiting for. The woman in the sparkling gown, draped in jewelry, manicured, made up, glamorous . . . The diva rising up into the spotlight.

Because this is who I am, right? The person I've become over all those years in the public eye, the dancer who became an actress who became a singer . . . who became a star. This is the Jennifer Lopez everyone expects, so this is the person I want to give to the world. The Hollywood star, poised onstage in an arena of screaming fans.

Like a movie scene, in the sweetest dreams, I have pictured us together . . .

—"WAITING FOR TONIGHT"

This was the scenario I wanted to create in the Big Hollywood opening section of the Dance Again tour: the emergence of the star, with all the glamour and glitz. It was life imitating art imitating life, and I

wanted to give everyone the full Hollywood treatment exactly as it had happened to me . . .

Big Hollywood would feature the big hits—"Get Right," "Love Don't Cost a Thing," "I'm Into You," and "Waiting for Tonight." And the truth was, we had been waiting for tonight, all of us, for a very long time. Through nine albums, through thirteen years, through all the ups and downs. Through whatever fears I'd felt about putting on this show, we were finally here.

It's perfect, it's passion, it's setting me free
From all of my sadness, the tears that I've cried
I have spent all of my life, waiting for tonight . . .

—"WAITING FOR TONIGHT"

A DREAM TO DANCE

Ever since I was a little girl, there were two things that came naturally to me: dancing and running. I can't remember a time before I did these things, and from the moment I started, I've never stopped doing either one of them.

I never wanted to slow down. Moving fast, moving forward is a natural state of being for me. When I was in junior high school, my younger sister went to try out for the track team. I tagged along and ended up getting chosen for the team myself. From then on, I ran every race and tried to win every medal and trophy that I could. Just running and running and running.

I love the feeling it gives me. I get into a rhythm that puts me in this meditative state, a zone where I feel powerful, strong, healthy, and calm. There's a great line that Lil Wayne raps during "I'm Into You." He says: "Every finish line is the beginning of a new race." That's how I've always felt, my whole life. Always rushing and hurrying—never wanting to sit still. As I would later find out, that's a useful trait to have when you're building a career, but it's not so great in building relationships.

okay now I'm into you, like you never knew
I'm falling for ya baby, I need a parachute.

—"I'M INTO YOU"

I wasn't one of those people who had some master plan to get to where I am today. When I was a little girl, I didn't think, *I'm going to be a star!* I trained hard and worked hard and I liked to win. But I never thought it would lead to where it did—not that I ever stopped to think about it, of course. (Who had time? I was running!)

Now dancing, I started when I was fourteen, in the neighborhood community center at the Kips Bay Boys & Girls Club. As with running, I became obsessive about it. Dancing had a similar rhythm to it, and it felt natural to me. It made me feel good and I was good at it. I practiced until my legs and feet ached—I wanted to be the best at it that I could possibly be.

I put in long hours. That's what my parents taught me to do when you had big dreams. I followed their example of working hard, and I put everything I had into it. I'd go to classes and rehearsals early to warm up first, and I stayed later than everyone else, going over a tough move or getting in one more practice. All I knew during those long days was that I loved what I was doing and maybe, just maybe, I could do it forever.

Being a professional dancer was my dream and I worked hard toward reaching that goal. But from when I was very little, I would close my eyes in bed at night and imagine that perfect family, with children and a husband who loved me above all else.

Throughout my life, I've had a few serious relationships. Each relationship was different and each relationship had its issues. But there was one thing they all had in common: They all had a passionate intensity that I mistook, every time, for my happily ever after. In each relationship, I thought my childhood fairy tale was coming to life, and that was all that mattered to me at the time.

Reality is hard to see through the adrenaline rush of a new love. It's easy to project your hopes and dreams onto a relationship when it's new and exciting, but the truth is that it is only in knowing who you are at your core and staying true to yourself that you can possibly see the difference between passion and real love.

I was lucky—or unlucky—enough to be with men who were really intense about their feelings for me. They did some crazy things, and I mean *crazy things*. Like releasing hundreds of doves outside my window, buying me a Bentley (or two), giving me rare diamonds, throwing me giant parties, or sending me private jets to sweep me off somewhere. I'm talking about grand gestures of love, passion, or whatever you want to call it. And I loved it. It was intoxicating when it was happening.

When a man does something like that, it's easy to think, *Wow, look how much he loves me!* I believed that these gestures inevitably signified love. *He's giving me gifts that I could only dream of, or putting up posters telling me how special I am all along the street where I drive to work. Does it get any better than this? Nobody has ever loved anybody as much as this guy loves me.*

But passion is a pendulum that swings both ways. As beautiful as it can be, it can also get very intense. Yet, through thick and thin, I chose to stay in those relationships. Because how can you turn your back on a love so big, so amazing, so real? The problem is, it wasn't real love; it was passion. I just didn't know the difference yet.

Passion is a pendulum that swings both ways. As beautiful as it can be, it can also get very intense.

I found myself in relationships that ended in hurt no matter how much I tried. I was always focused on one thing. I always tried to be the perfect girlfriend, the perfect wife. I felt like I was doing my best, so why weren't things working out?

BECOMING SOMEONE ELSE

Throughout the turmoil in my personal life, and some heartbreaking disappointments in love, I continued to work hard in my career, putting all of my energy into new music and new movie projects. At some point along the way, I was no longer Jennifer from the Bronx, I was becoming Jennifer Lopez, the conglomerate. Now I was J.Lo "the brand."

Talk about running! I was in full stride. People were taking me seriously, as both an actress and a singer. I was living out my dreams, the dreams I had fallen asleep to while sharing a bed with my two sisters in our small Bronx apartment, exhausted after a day of dance classes. I was

pouring my heart and soul into my career. I had honest intentions and I worked hard.

But there was still that other dream of a loving family, and unlike my career, where all the pieces were falling beautifully into place, love remained a puzzle that I couldn't find the right pieces for—the one thing I didn't seem able to figure out. I still wanted desperately to find "the one"—the man I'd settle down and spend my life with.

As I sat there envisioning the opening section for the first part of the tour, thinking about that time in my life, something happened. I was hit with the first of many realizations I was to have throughout the process of putting the show together: All that running I was doing in my career, I was doing in my relationships too. I had never stopped to take a look at that before.

I rushed into each relationship with optimism and hope, always thinking I'd found what I was looking for. And I was always disappointed when they ended, wondering what went wrong.

FOOLED BY LOVE

I think back to Lynda and Leslie and me, sandwiched together for all those years . . . I loved my sisters. I still do. I didn't mind a bit that we were all up in one another's space, even at night when we were sleeping.

But then, once my career took off and I was in the middle of the whirlwind of this Hollywood fairy tale, my life was so different. I was now staying in beautiful hotels and huge penthouse suites . . . Paradise, right? I was a grown-up now, out there on my own, traveling and seeing the world, and yet I couldn't stand sleeping by myself; I was always looking for another person to be with me. It wasn't that I *preferred* to be with someone else—the problem was, I hated not to be. You have to be okay on your own before you can have a healthy relationship with another person, but again, I didn't know that yet.

You have to be okay
on your own before
you can have a healthy
relationship with another
person.

I was never single for long, and whenever I got together with some-one, that was it—we were instantly inseparable, monogamous, together for the long haul. I never thought, *Well, let me take some time to see if I really want to be with this person. Do I even like him? Is he right for me?* I didn't see this behavior for what it was—an act of not really loving myself.

I'm about to sign you up, we can get right
Before the night is up, we can get
get right get right, we can get
right

—"GET RIGHT"

THE START OF MY FAIRY TALE

Sometimes love strikes when you're least expecting it. Marc came back into my life three days after I should have been at the altar saying "I do" to another man. With Marc, unlike my other relationships, I found common ground and similar dreams, instead of passion, at first. I thought I could build something real with him, something that would last.

It was the total opposite of the relationship I was coming out of. Be-ing a couple that was on the cover of every tabloid magazine for two years straight, hounded by the paparazzi and constantly judged—our relationship crumbled under the pressures of the media scrutiny that surrounded us. Ben Affleck and I called off our wedding, ending our very public relationship in suitably dramatic fashion just days before we were to walk down the aisle of a fairy-tale wedding we had planned for months. It was just the cover of a magazine or a headline to everyone else—today's joke, tomorrow's trash—but for me, when Ben and I split up at the moment when I thought we were committing to each other forever, it was my first real heartbreak, it felt like my heart had been torn out of my chest. And when the realization that I wasn't going to have the fairy tale family I wanted really set in, well, that was when I really started to fall apart. I was dealing with the emotional pain of all that buildup and letdown, the high hopes and excitement that ended in tears and frustration.

People do lots of things to anesthetize themselves in moments like these. Some people do drugs, some drink, and some go out and party. I get that, but I've never been one to do those things. No, my way of anesthetizing the pain was different. I sought out comfort in another person, tried to find someone who could make me feel loved and wanted in my loneliest hour.

And that was the moment when Marc reappeared in my life.

Marc and I had been friends for a number of years. We'd worked together on a few songs, and we'd sung a duet together for my first record, titled "*No Me Ames*" (ironically, "Don't Love Me" in Spanish). Right from the beginning, he never made it a secret that he liked me. He was warm and funny, a brilliant singer and artist who knew how to make me feel special. But the best thing about him, the thing that I loved the most, was that no matter what, he always knew how to make me laugh. I had always liked Marc, finding comfort in his humor and his easy way with people. He was confident and strong, he was so sure of everything, and at this moment, when I felt so lost, so broken and alone, there he was.

We thought that this was where everything was supposed to lead, that we were meant to end up together. All the heartache and pain of my recent breakup couldn't have been for nothing, could it? Maybe I had to go through the bad so I could end up with the person I was meant to be with all along.

After all, the first time I ever met Marc in 1998, backstage while he was performing on Broadway, his opening line to me had been: "One day you're going to be my wife." (True story.)

We make our own choices . . . and I chose to believe that Marc and I were meant to be together—that destiny was stepping in. In that mo-

ment, I needed to believe that; I needed to believe in something. The reality was, I didn't want to be alone—so when Marc was there, when he met me with his big smile, his heart on his sleeve, and his arms open wide, I was more than happy to let myself fall into them. I had always liked him, but now that he was coming to my rescue in my time of need, he was my knight in shining armor and I realized I loved him too. This had to be the start of my fairy tale.

And from there, it didn't take long for us to decide to get married.

Thinking back, maybe deep down I knew that this was a Band-Aid on the cut, that my wound hadn't been stitched or healed. But I pushed all that to the back of my mind. Because life takes unpredictable twists and turns, right? And you've just got to go with what you feel is best in the moment.

In that moment, Marc was the guy who swooped in and made me feel loved at my lowest point. I loved him for that, and I felt like I could love him forever. After all the turmoil, I felt like I had found my rock, the man whom I was going to spend the rest of my life with.

I think you need to take some time

To show me that your love is true

—"LOVE DON'T COST A THING"

FINDING STRENGTH BEYOND YOUR LIMITS

When we first started doing rehearsals for the Dance Again tour, my body almost couldn't take it. Dancing all the time, working on all these different moves, different set pieces . . . Oh my God, I was so sore at

the end of each day. My muscles were tight, my whole body was aching, and I'd kneel on the floor in the shower and let the water beat down on my back.

I knew if I pushed through the pain, my body would get used to it. And soon I would get stronger, and feel better, and get to be in amazing shape. Because once you build up that strength and stamina, you end up feeling better than you ever could have imagined. By the end of a tour, you feel like you can jump over buildings. But to get to that point, first you have to push through the pain.

That's kind of how I approached my relationship with Marc. I never thought, *Maybe I rushed into this*, or *Maybe we're not the best people for each other. Maybe I made a mistake. Maybe we were too different*. I wouldn't let myself think that. I couldn't. Instead, I tried to convince myself that it was all going to work out fine if I could push through the rough spot.

I think of the days when the sun

used to set

On my empty heart all alone in my

bed

Tossing and turning, emotions

were strong

I knew I had to hold on

—"WAITING FOR TONIGHT"

Marc and I weren't the only ones who really wanted this marriage to work. Our fans were invested in it too. They wanted to see it last. Marrying Marc was like the happy ending, the twist in the story that turned me back in people's minds from J.Lo the Diva to Jennifer Lopez, married woman. "Bennifer" was gone, and now there was just Marc and Jennifer, the couple that was meant to be. I didn't want to give that up.

Because now I had lined up everything I needed for the perfect Big Hollywood life—the movies, the records, the glamour—and now the marriage that would really last forever, with the man who rescued me when I was lost.

During this whole period of my life, everything felt like a hurricane, and that's how I wanted the opening of the show to feel. It was exciting and moving and loud . . . and it was scary.

I knew people wanted to see the same dancing and choreography they'd seen in the videos for all these songs—so that's what we gave them, but with bigger arrangements, more dancers, a bigger stage, so it felt to the audience how it felt to me. We were taking something old and making it exciting and fresh. It was the perfect opening. Our eight male dancers started out in those classic tuxedos, with top hats and canes,

dancing like they'd stepped out of a Fred Astaire movie. But then, as we moved deeper into the set, the tone began to change.

Little by little, the hats came off, the jackets came off, and then the shirts came off too. We started to literally bare ourselves here. Now there were eight shirtless guys in bow ties and slacks, and the mood started changing. It was about to get . . . interesting.

That's when we go to what Ana—one of my best friends and the photographer for the Dance Again tour—called "the fainting transition" of the show: "Waiting for Tonight" accompanied by a beautiful, electrifying laser show. This was where things got very sexy and a little dangerous. All these elements combined created an intense atmosphere. Whenever we performed this part of the show, people started falling out left and right, fainting in front of the stage, right in front of me as I sang.

Every night, I would see them fall, and they'd be carried off and revived backstage. At first it freaked me out—Big Hollywood was out of control! And the funny thing is, that seemed right. Because that was how it had felt in real life . . .

ACT TWO

BACK TO THE BRONX

SET LIST

"Goin' In"

———

The BX medley: "I'm Real," "All I Have," "Feelin' So Good," "Ain't It Funny"

———

"Jenny from the Block"

———

I lost some confidence. I almost lost my way.

I had to go home—to my roots, my

upbringing, my inspiration.

That's where I found the answer.

JENNY FROM THE BLOCK

REDISCOVERING DANCE

I had given the audience the big glamorous Hollywood-movie-star opening. That's how the world saw me. But where was I to go from there? To answer that question, I had to ask myself, *Who am I really?* I knew, but for the show, I had to revisit the place that inspired my passion: Castle Hill Avenue in the Bronx. That was my neighborhood, the place where I grew up hearing hip-hop, salsa, R&B, pop, and every other kind of beat, all while walking down the block. Our neighbors were so diverse—Puerto Ricans, Dominicans, African-Americans, Italians and Irish—and everybody was scraping and clawing, trying to get by.

My mom worked two jobs and my dad worked the night shift at Guardian Insurance. My sisters, Leslie and Lynda, and I shared a bed, and every morning we were bundled up and sent off to Catholic school. That was why my parents worked all those long hours, so they could pay for a good education and raise us right. I can still remember those days of walking to school at seven a.m., freezing in my little uniform skirt and kneesocks, the snow dusting the streets.

We used to dance and sing together, my sisters and I, putting on little shows in the living room. We did it because we loved it, because it was fun to act like we were on a stage somewhere. You could get so much material just walking down the street, seeing people and what they were wearing, and going into stores and listening to them talk. The Bronx was alive with sound and color and life, and I soaked it all up.

You could get so much material just walking down the street, seeing people and what they were wearing, and going into stores and listening to them talk. The Bronx was alive with sound and color and life, and we soaked it all up.

I grew up in the age of hip-hop, and I remember being in elementary school the first time I heard "Rapper's Delight" by the Sugarhill Gang. That song changed my world—I was like, "Play it again! Play it again! PLAY IT AGAIN!" I had never heard anything like it before, and it was so cool. It felt like the heartbeat of my upbringing, the soundtrack to my life. I always identified with that beat, the grit and the pulse of it.

Years later, I sang about those times in the song "Feelin' So Good," and the video took me right back to Castle Hill.

when I opened up my eyes today
Felt the sun shining on my face . . .

—"FEELIN' SO GOOD"

It was Big Pun and Fat Joe and me, all of us back in the Bronx, singing about the pleasures of everyday life there . . . simple pleasures like walking into the beauty parlor, picking up your check, and buying yourself something new to wear so you could go out with your friends and have fun. I remember those times, the feeling that endless possibility existed in even the smallest things.

Those were moments I'd think back to later on, whenever the hard times knocked me flat. Whenever I'd go through a breakup, when I'd feel like I was losing myself, I'd find myself thinking, *You need to get back to who you are.* And then I'd wonder, *Well, who am I?* Was there something missing from back in the days when I was that girl pounding the streets of New York, doing auditions and hoping for the big break?

Because that girl never worried about what the future was going to hold. I was always in the present, always knowing somehow that things were going to work out. Life was visceral; there was that Bronx mental-

ity of taking each day as it comes. I'd get up and go to dance class, then go to an audition, meet up with friends, and then choreograph something for a little show we were going to do. It was about pressing forward every day. I was relentless, reaching, always reaching, trying to get that brass ring. Nothing was going to stop me.

There was a certain hustle I grew up with, a hustle that I learned from watching my parents. They showed me that you put your head down and work—you work for a living and then, when you're making a living, you still don't stop. That continues to be my mentality now. We don't stop working because we have money in the bank—we do what we do and we keep on doing it. That's the way I was raised.

You put your head down and work—you work for a living and then, when you're making a living, you still don't stop.

And that's what keeps me grounded. It's real life, people surviving, people working hard to support their families. There might be some who see me as this person who's been privileged forever. But my first record didn't come out until I was twenty-eight years old. So for more than half of my life, I was out there struggling like everyone else for a chance to make it.

That's what "Jenny from the Block" is all about. That's what I wanted to show people in the Back to the Bronx section of the show, the duality between Big Hollywood and life on Castle Hill. Because yes, there's a public image that I enjoy—I love dressing up. I love feeling glamorous. I love jewelry and beautiful things. But I'm still that little girl who's playing the part of a movie star, that same girl from the Bronx wearing big hoop earrings and listening to hip-hop.

FIGHTING THROUGH THE PAIN

There's a boxing ring set up at center stage. And I'm a boxer, walking out into the spotlight with my corner men, who hold the ropes for me as I step into the ring. I'm wearing loose-fitting pants, a bikini top, and a black cape with a hood over my head. I turn around so the crowd can see the word stenciled across my back: LOVE?

I shadowbox for a few seconds as the dancers, in boxing trunks, join me in the ring. And then I pull the hood off my head, an announcer booms, "The champ is *here!*" . . . and everybody goes nuts.

You think you know who I am? You think I'm just that sparkly, feathery, bejeweled woman you see on the screen? Well, think again. The music kicks up, and . . . I'm *Goin' In!*

Tonight feels like we can do
anything we like
Tonight feels like the best night of
my life
I'm goin' in . . .

—"GOIN' IN"

I wanted to follow up the Big Hollywood opening with the Back to the Bronx section, to show people who I really was, that girl with the New York fight in me—and I knew exactly who could make that happen. I had seen some clips from a New Zealand choreographer named Parris Goebel, and her stuff was so tough—girls dancing like guys, leaving it all on the floor, and everything infused with this amazing energy. She was perfect.

Parris was never formally trained—she taught herself to dance and went from there to choreography, creating a style she called "polyswagg." She and her crew were world-champion hip-hop dancers, but she had never been hired for a show the size of the Dance Again tour. No one out there was doing what she was doing, so we gave Parris her first shot, knowing that she'd create something completely different from anything else we had seen onstage. And she *killed it.*

Once again, the show became life imitating art, imitating life, because

we went in with this whole boxing thing—you're down but not out, and no matter what's happening in your life, you keep fighting.

After performing in music videos and some of the biggest award shows in the world, performing night after night in front of tens of thousands of people on a world tour—despite what I imagined—proved to be one of the most natural things that I had ever done. That stage felt like home. All the nerves went away, and much like with running and dancing, I had clarity and I was in the moment. And this Bronx section in particular became my own personal daily affirmation of how, when you fall down, you have to get back up.

I would hold out the microphone and ask the audience every night: "Do you know where I'm from?"

And they'd scream back: "The Bronx!"

Then I'd say, "That's right. I'm just a simple girl from the Bronx."

They would laugh at the irony of me standing there wearing a track-suit that was covered head-to-toe in sparkly Swarovski crystals. Any-thing but simple.

"Is that how you do it here in Sydney? When you fall down, you get back up?" I asked.

And the crowd would go crazy.

"That's how we do it where I'm from. Can I ask you a question? Do you all want to go back to the Bronx with me?" I'd scream.

The crowd would erupt with a thunderous roar. *Waaaahhhhhhhhhh.* It was one of the most beautiful, empowering, and electrifying moments of the show.

At this point, pretty much everyone in the world knew that I had recently gone through a divorce, and night after night they were helping me get back up again. Maybe I was helping them too.

The night I shouted this out to the fans in the Boston TD Garden arena, I put on my sparkly New York Yankees ball cap, like I did every night. And everybody started booing—of course! Die-hard Red Sox fans, what are you gonna do?

As they booed, I started laughing. And they all started cracking up too, and soon we were all laughing together. I shrugged my shoulders and said, "I got to wear it wherever I go, you know? I can't not be from New York today." I am who I am, no matter where life takes me.

No matter where I go
I know where I came from . . .

—"JENNY FROM THE BLOCK"

The stage is set, guys carrying boom boxes and hanging out on their bikes, girls wearing hot shorts sitting on beach chairs in front of chain-link fences, video content filled with graffiti and the six train running through the city . . . That's how we set the stage for this pulsating urban section of the show. No matter what city around the world we were visiting, at that moment everybody knew we were back in the Bronx.

Certain songs fell perfectly into this part of the show. "I'm Real," "Ain't It Funny," "Feelin' So Good," "Jenny from the Block"—they had become so much a part of my image, how people saw me, because that's how I saw myself. I always felt like I was this tough girl from the

streets who knew what was what and wouldn't take shit from anybody. The girl who had her head on straight and knew exactly what she wanted. Who would never let herself be treated like dirt, who would never lose herself in a relationship, who would never feel her whole world shaken by anyone . . .

Was I really still that girl?

I always thought so, but then I remembered a conversation from years ago, back in the beginning of my career. I was in a meeting with my agent and stepped out for a call with my boyfriend at the time. Through the glass door, my agent could see that I was arguing and pleading. She asked my assistant, "Does Jennifer have low self-esteem?" My assistant looked at her like she was crazy. Later, when my assistant told me she had said that, we couldn't stop laughing. Me? Low self-esteem? "That's so stupid!" I told her. But was it really? That agent saw something I didn't. She was a little bit older. Maybe she'd been through something like that herself, or maybe she'd seen it in others. Who knows what? All that mattered was, she knew it when she saw it in me.

ACCEPTING MY FATE

Now I know I'm not perfect, but I know I was a good girlfriend, a good wife. I tried my best. I always put up that old Bronx fight! I went to the mat for every relationship I was in. I asked myself the hard questions: How can *I* fix things? What can *I* do to make the other person happier? Or, How can *I* take care of their needs? I was asking myself all these questions—they seemed like the right questions—but for some reason it still didn't work out.

My life might have continued on like that forever, but then everything changed in 2008, when I had my beautiful babies, Emme and Max.

Marc and I had been trying to have kids ever since we got married. We never worried about birth control, figuring that nature would take its course and soon enough I would get pregnant. But the first few years of our marriage were kinda shaky, and with the stress of that, nothing happened. While at first it didn't seem like a big deal, later on I began to worry.

After three years of marriage, our relationship had settled down a bit, and my career was kind of in a lull. I'd released a record that wasn't my best one, and I hadn't done a movie in a while. It was this strange in-between time. All my focus was on my marriage, and it felt like the right time to have kids—but I wasn't getting pregnant. Marc already had three kids by two other women, so I began to think it was about me. *Maybe this isn't going to happen,* I thought.

Right as I started thinking that way, I had a conversation with my dad while he was visiting one Sunday afternoon. "Things are going pretty well with Marc and me," I told him. "And it's not like we haven't been trying to get pregnant. But it's not happening. I don't know. Maybe I'm not meant to have kids. I mean, I have this amazing career, wonderful friends, lots of extended family . . . Maybe that's asking for too much. I guess my life is going to be about other things—my work and career—rather than having kids," I told my dad.

And then he said something that was so simple and yet so profound that it stopped me in my tracks: "Well, why can't you have both?"

It sounded like such a practical question, but when my dad said it out loud, it was like the wall I had created for myself with my insecurities and feelings of unworthiness cracked open and the light came through. I was able to see that I deserved to have that blessing as much as anybody else. No matter what happened, I could do this.

Everything I'd been telling myself about having kids and having a career came out of the fear that I wasn't really worthy, that I didn't deserve it. That I already had so much. It came straight out of a lack of love for myself. But my dad put it so simply: *Why can't you?* And for the first time ever, I truly believed that I could.

The very next month, I got pregnant. It was almost as if I had to make the decision that it *could* happen before it did. But even when it did happen, I couldn't believe it. It took seven pregnancy tests before reality would set in. And then seven weeks later I found out I wasn't having only one baby but two. Twins! All I could do was laugh; all Marc could do was cry . . . tears of happiness.

Oh my God. I was *really* pregnant.

BECOMING A MOM IN FRONT OF THE WORLD

Six months into my pregnancy, I was scheduled to open the Movies Rock 2007 show, where Marc was also scheduled to perform. I was backstage with Marc as the show was about to begin. This was going to be my first real public appearance with my very pregnant belly, so I was a little nervous. As I walked out onstage, the first thing you saw was a gigantic belly draped in a white Versace dress, and people started clapping. They liked this Jennifer—the married woman, pregnant with twins, all safe and nice, rather than wild Jennifer, running around in clubs. It's funny—when you're single and out there doing your thing, people feel okay making you a target. But when you're somebody's wife, somebody's mom, then they back off a little bit on criticizing you. It was new for me and it was nice.

People kept clapping, and soon everyone was on their feet. I felt like it was the babies' first standing ovation, because people were clapping not only for me, but for the three of us! It was a very warm welcome to motherhood, and I was soaking it up. It felt like the first step toward redefining myself in the public eye as a mama. This was going to be the role of a lifetime.

TAKING A STAND

Any mom will tell you that becoming a mother is one of the most life-changing experiences you will have. My babies changed me in so many ways and even before they were born I started to notice the ways in which I started to see life differently.

There was one incident in particular that made me realize just how much they were changing me. When I was about six months pregnant, I was at an event and someone standing near me lit up a cigarette. Now, I've been around smokers my whole life and while it's not something I enjoy, cigarette smoke had never bothered me before.

But now I was pregnant. I didn't want to be inhaling the smoke, so I moved away from them. It was such a small thing, but it got me thinking: I've been around smokers before, but it never bothered me. I never even thought about the effect it had on me. But now someone lights up a cigarette and I don't hesitate a second to move as far away as possible because I'm worried it will affect my babies . . . Why did I never think about that for myself? Why were my health and well-being not important? I loved these babies so much. I didn't want anything to harm them in any way. Did I not hold myself in the same regard?

I realized that being pregnant, of course, wasn't only about me anymore; I had two other people to take care of. But in order to take care of them, I needed to take care of myself. In fact, I always needed to take care of myself, I had just never thought about it before!

This was a different Jennifer. Before, I might get frustrated at something someone had done but I'd swallow my feelings and move on. But now, because of the babies, I was thinking differently, and I was going to do what I thought was right for them, and for me. And I wasn't about to compromise.

It was a step, a tiny step, in the right direction. I was finally starting to behave in a way that was putting me and my twins first. It might seem like a small little thing, but this incident led to a big realization of how I was mistreating myself. That was the first of many ways in which my babies changed me, and there were more changes to come.

No matter how strong and self-confident I thought I was, I had ignored when things didn't feel right. In reality, I was accepting things I didn't want.

It was easy to blame other people for treating me in ways I didn't like, but now I was seeing that I was the one at fault. The only way you can be mistreated is by allowing yourself to be mistreated, and that was something I did over and over again. Somehow, I needed to find that glimmer of self-respect, buried deep inside, that would allow me to say: *I am never going to let that happen to me again.* I needed to learn how to stand up for myself in a different way, but I didn't know how.

So, here I was, that girl from the Bronx, fighting and fighting like I was supposed to . . . but who was I really fighting against?

"I'm still, I'm still Jenny from the block"

—"JENNY FROM THE BLOCK"

Back to the Bronx was one of the most popular moments in the show because it was nostalgic. It took people back to that old-school hip-hop feeling, back to that time when you felt like you knew everything, to that hip-hop cockiness that made you feel so powerful, like you could take over the world and nobody was going to get the best of you.

The only way you can be mistreated is by allowing yourself to be mistreated.

As energetic as that moment was onstage, while I was putting it all together, the realizations were coming fast and furious. Performing it every night was reminding me of so many past missteps but also of the essence of who I really was. I might have lost my way, but Jenny from the Block was still alive and well. She was still in there.

ACT THREE

FUNKY LOVE

The dawn of a new day.

I rekindled the feeling that I had something to

offer to the world.

For the first time in a long time, I felt closer to

myself.

FUNKY LOVE

OBSESSED WITH LOVE

Over the years, love has been a constant theme in my music. I always knew this, but it was never clearer to me than when looking through my albums while putting the show together. I realized that over seven studio albums, I have more than sixty songs about love or with the word "love" in the title: "If You Had My Love," "Could This Be Love," "*No Me Ames*," "Love Don't Cost a Thing," "I Need Love," "I, Love," "Baby I Love U!" "Loving You," et cetera, et cetera, et cetera. Wow. Even I surprised myself on that one. I guess I really had a lot to say on the topic; I was really trying to figure this thing out.

So now, in the show, after having gone from Hollywood to the Bronx, the Funky Love section would get to the heart of who I was as an artist. Love has always been my message. Love in all its glory, the good and the bad—wanting to get it right, always wanting, always hoping, always fighting. It's about that passion that's so intoxicating, and it can be as healing as it can be destructive.

This is what my music has always been about: being in love. Love love love love love. So we decided to kick this section off with "Hold It Don't Drop It," a retro R&B–flavored song that ironically—or not so ironically—is about not wanting to leave or give up on somebody. I wanted it to be half James Brown, half Tina Turner. So for this section, Zuhair Murad, who created the costumes for the entire show, designed a short, fringy, electric-blue dress with a floor-length maribou cape. I came out shaking my hips and thrashing my hair as the band pounded out the soulful throwback. There were three male dancers in the most sparkly, sequined suits that you've ever seen. They were like the Pips, dancing funk-inspired choreography and killing it dead. I sang in my grittiest voice about how I wasn't going to leave, and it ended with the guys literally having to drag me off the stage, picking me up and throwing me over their shoulders as the band banged out the encore over and over until I finally gave up. It was metaphoric, I guess, for how reluctantly I would leave relationships, and never without a fight.

Every time I try to run, something
keeps stopping me,
I try my best to turn around, but
your touch won't let me leave.

—"HOLD IT DON'T DROP IT"

From there, we would slow it way down. We had to, after that. I'd say to the audience, "I know I get carried away with love sometimes. It ain't no secret. You guys want to talk about love? I have a lot of stories!"

They'd giggle. So would I. And that's how we took them into the first real intimate moment of the show, an acoustic version of "If You Had My Love."

"If You Had My Love" was my very first single from my very first album, a kind of defining song for me. I wanted to do it really pared down, so it would feel like a conversation—like I'm talking with the audience, sharing where I began and where I find myself now. The lyrics are all about the beginning of a new relationship and what I expect and what I want. And there's a little bit of fear in there too, a feeling of, *What will you do if I give you my heart?*

In the verses, I'm trying to lay down the rules, but the chorus expresses all of the fear that I feel . . .

If you had my love and I gave you all my trust,
Would you comfort me?

Love has always been my message. Love in all its glory, the good and the bad.

After finishing the song, I'd look out at everybody and say, "That was the very first song I ever sang about love . . ." And every single night as I said it, the feelings and weight of all my experiences were right there in that phrase. "A lot has happened since then." Again, we shared a laugh, because they knew what I was talking about . . . Because we've all been through it, right? I wanted to have that moment with them, to show that we've all been on this journey together. From the stage I could always see people nodding and smiling. They knew exactly what I meant the moment I said it.

It was my way of saying, *Yeah, I'm up here onstage, but I'm human. And this is one area that I can't seem to get right for some reason.* It's the moment in the show where I start to bare my soul.

What was amazing about doing that, night after night on the tour, was that every time I did it, I felt a little bit more forgiving of myself. There's something liberating about standing up in front of a crowd of people and saying, *I know that maybe I haven't made the best choices. Maybe things haven't always worked out. But I'm right here and I'm saying it. I'm not ashamed, and I'm still trying.* In doing that, I discovered that sometimes it helps to make yourself vulnerable. The people, the songs, and the show were helping me to learn to forgive myself and accept myself for who I was, mistakes and all. Little by little I was healing.

After the babies were born, as I embraced my strength and regained my sense of self, I began to look around and take stock of the rest of my life, including my career and my relationships. I was on the road toward trusting my instincts, following my own heart, and I was beginning to see things more clearly. Once all of the other aspects of my life were in order, those that weren't became impossible to ignore.

One of the areas of my life that fulfilled me during that time was being a judge on *American Idol*. It was a surprising safe haven during some very rocky times, and it profoundly changed my life.

When I first got the call to do *Idol*, it seemed like no one around me thought it was a good idea. A lot of things were in transition—Max and Emme were toddlers, my music and my acting were still in a lull, and I was concentrating on my family, traveling with Marc while he toured. It was a strange time, and I thought that doing *Idol* would be a new challenge, something different. Everyone around me seemed to think that doing a reality TV show would be some kind of comedown for me. For the most part, they urged me not to do it. But I disagreed.

"We're in a new era," I told them. "Television is the new radio. It's how people get music." For some reason, I knew it would be okay. I knew doing the show would bring other benefits too. I wanted to be home with Max and Emme, who were only two at the time, and working on *American Idol*, which shoots mostly in Los Angeles, would make that possible. I could make good money and stay put with my family. It seemed like it would be fun too. I really loved the show and believed that I had something to contribute to it. There were so many things about doing the show that I knew would be good. But I never imagined how much more, not only professionally but personally, *American Idol* would do for me.

When I was asked to do the show, I thought I was in a really good place. I was enjoying having a family and I loved being a mommy. This was so different from anything I'd done before. Would I really be up for this? *Come on!* I was a mom now. I could do anything! I had just birthed two human beings—from my belly!

I remember that day so clearly. The day that Max and Emme were born. The first time I saw them, I was in the hospital, lying on that table, having my C-section, and my doctor shouted: "Baby number one on the left!"

I looked, and there was Emme, arms outstretched, legs shaking, a little purple creature screaming at the top of her lungs, "*Waaaaaaaaa!*"

Then someone said, "Baby number two on the right!" I looked again and "*Waaaaaaaaa!*"—another little purple creature, screaming even louder: That was my Max.

I reached out and pulled them to my chest, and all I remember was kissing them and saying, *I love you. I love you. I love you so much. I love you . . .* It was instinctual. It was pure. It was unconditional. *This* was love—a love I had never felt before. It empowered me in a way that I could have never imagined.

This was love—a love I had never felt before. It empowered me in a way that I could have never imagined.

Naturally, after I had children, my life became about them. Suddenly, there are these two little beings who are totally dependent on you, who literally can't live without you. It's so easy to lose yourself in that beautiful world when you have babies. It's magical and all encompassing.

So three years later, when the chance to do *Idol* came up, I welcomed the opportunity to reclaim some of my individuality. I needed to quiet all the voices in order to listen to my own, and to trust what I felt was right in order to make a decision. I followed my gut and jumped in.

When I first began working on the show—several months before it started airing—I fell in love with Steven Tyler, Randy Jackson, and Ryan Seacrest. They were all very different, but each one was so caring and generous—they all really looked out for me. They were like the brothers I never had. When I'd come onto the set, Steven would say, "Jennifer! You look gorgeous—what do you use on your face?" He always wanted to know what makeup I was using, what hair products. He made me laugh so much, always saying, "You know I'm only asking because I'm so *enamored* with you; I'm very *enamored* with you, Jennifer," with that wry smile on his face.

Steven was nothing like what you'd think. People think he's this skinny, crazy rocker, with that larger-than-life mouth and the wild clothes. But he's so deep, so soulful. When you look into his eyes, he's like a little wounded bird. He likes to lock eyes, in that un-self-conscious way of someone who loves to connect with people.

He'd look at me, and I'd see a little bit of sadness in those eyes, a little bit of pain in a way that made me know, *Yeah, that guy has lived.* He had a soulfulness; he was good a person. You could see it.

Those first few weeks, as we shot the auditions and met all these amazing young singers, who were fantastic, we got to know one another too. I loved working with the guys, and I felt good about what I was able to contribute.

When I saw the clips from those first audition shows, I thought they looked great. *Idol* had been slumping a little bit in the last couple of seasons, but if everything went well, twenty million people would be tuning in to watch us. How could things get any better?

STEPPING ONTO A BIG STAGE

It was the middle of the night, and Marc was asleep beside me in bed. I suddenly sat upright, my heart pounding. It was the night before my debut on the premiere of *American Idol.* I slipped out of bed and walked into the bathroom, and when I looked at myself in the mirror, I was as white as a ghost. All I could think was, *Oh shit. Twenty million people.* I was so nervous about the show airing the next day that I was completely freaking out.

I came back to bed and said, "Marc! Wake up!" He was in a deep sleep, so he kind of grunted and rolled over. I said, "Papi! Wake up! I'm scared!" I grabbed his shoulder and tried to shake him awake. "You gotta wake up!"

No matter what problems Marc and I had in our personal lives, we were always very in tune with each other when it came to work. When I was worried that my singing wasn't as strong as other things I was able to do, he helped me find my best singing voice. I really credit him with that, because he always encouraged me, giving me tips and telling me I could do it. And he always had a really smart take on things when it came to business—he was a wonderful partner in that sense. So, if anyone could talk me down from this ledge, it was him.

"Baby," I said, "I am freaking out."

"What's wrong?" he asked, his voice groggy with sleep.

"It's this whole *Idol* thing," I said. "It's so big! Twenty million people are going to be watching, and I've never done TV like this, without a script or lyrics or anything . . . It's only me out there, with the cameras and everybody watching!"

I felt like I'd be exposed, vulnerable—like I'd be running down the street with no clothes on. It's not that I was afraid of people seeing the real me. I knew who I was; I knew I was a good person. But this was new for me. When you're an actress, you're used to saying lines that someone has given you. You get to hide behind that mask. When you're a singer, you have a song. The notion of getting up in front of everyone and being yourself is really terrifying. If someone criticizes your acting, they're criticizing only one part of you. They don't know anything about who you really are or what's really important to you. If someone criticizes you on a show like *Idol*, though, they're criticizing *you*.

"Okay, okay," he said. "But that's not so bad. Think about how you'd feel if it failed. What if no one was watching . . . ? That would be so much worse, right?"

I thought about that for a second and then said, "Yeah, that would feel worse."

And with that, we both rolled over and went to sleep.

I had to laugh, because Marc was right. Did it make sense to be scared because the show was potentially a huge success? No . . . But it was really just that number—twenty million people—that threw me off. With television, people can flip through channels, and then suddenly they see you sitting on that judging panel—and now you're the one getting judged by every one of those people who've just happened to tune in. You're being scrutinized on a whole different level. And that was a really overwhelming thought.

But Marc knew exactly how to calm me down. He knew that what I feared more than any of those things was failure. "Listen, if the show failed, *then* you'd feel really shitty," he said, and he was right. Because I

know what it feels like to fail, to have something that you've worked really hard on, something that you care about, be judged a failure. Trust me, I have had that experience. And for me, there's no worse feeling than putting something out there that people don't respond to.

But when the show started airing, something wonderful happened. The very thing I was afraid of turned out to be the best thing ever: For the first time, people were seeing the real me—not the "me" fabricated by tabloids and magazines—and they liked what they saw.

BACK TO THE REAL ME

The truth about reality TV is that you can't hide who you are. When you're sitting up there on a panel, reacting to the performers you see in front of you, the camera catches everything. If you start laughing, if you shed tears, if you make a face—it's all right there for the world to see. When people started watching that season of *American Idol*, they were seeing something they weren't expecting to see. People were looking for a diva, but they found the mama instead.

Of all the good things I thought might come out of being on *Idol*, this one I hadn't expected—and it turned out to be the biggest, most important thing of all. It had been so long since I'd felt like just . . . Jennifer.

Before *Idol* started, I was hanging out with my friend Leah. She's my bestie, we have real love for each other, we connected instantly, from the first day we met. It doesn't matter what I say or how out there I think it is, she always gets it. We get each other. I remember saying to her, "I feel like I'm about to have a baby. Like, I'm pregnant and I'm pushing, and I'm feeling the pain, but it's not quite out yet. But there's this beautiful baby coming . . ." It was strange, but that's how I felt it at the time . . . like I was on the precipice of something amazing. I could feel it coming, even if I wasn't totally sure of what it was.

So many exciting things were starting to happen. People were loving the show. I had a new album coming out, and when "On the Floor," the first single, leaked right before *Idol* aired, it shot up the charts. It seemed like every day something great and new came along. I felt an amazing new energy in my life and career, the kind of energy I hadn't felt in a long time.

In so many ways, *Idol* was like a reinvention, a reintroduction into the public eye for me. I was finding my own voice, my own power again—I had something to say, and people were listening. It was the first time in a long time that I felt good about just being me. And the response to being

The truth about reality TV is that you can't hide who you are.

me, not only from Steven and Randy and Ryan and everyone at *Idol*, but also from the audience watching the show, was so warm and embracing that I felt protected and loved. It got me back in touch with myself.

That was a really big deal for me. It gave me back a little bit of the self-confidence I had lost over time, a little bit of the grounding I had been lacking since the Big Hollywood whirlwind took over my life. I hadn't even realized how much self-confidence I'd lost until it finally started coming back.

All of this happened gradually, over the course of that first *American Idol* season. It wasn't a "Eureka!" kind of moment—it was the slow realization that the parts of me that had been empty were starting to fill up again. Yet, as gradual as this all was, there was one surreal moment that crystallized it for me—one moment where I suddenly understood what *Idol* meant to people and what it was doing for me.

It happened during Oscar season, when the show had been on the air for about a month. I had been invited to a party celebrating one of the movies up for Best Picture, and so I got dressed up and went out to do that Hollywood thing. There are always lots of big stars at these parties—actors and directors and heads of studios, the people who make things happen in this town. I pretty much expected to blend in and have a good time, but when I walked into the party, people started swarming all around me, asking about *American Idol*.

It was unreal . . . People were coming up, saying things like, "Oh my God! I love you on that show!" And "Who do you think is going to win? Come on. Tell the truth!" And, "What's it really like behind the scenes? What's the scoop?" I couldn't believe that in this room full of the most successful, creative people in Hollywood, everyone wanted to talk about *Idol*. I mean, even Steven Spielberg came up to me to tell me about how he and his family all watch the show together. Steven Spielberg!

Wow. The power of TV.

At that moment, I realized how much people liked the show, how happy it made them feel, and how much it was changing the perception of who I was. People were saying they liked me, which made me realize how many years I'd spent thinking they didn't, and that affected how I felt about myself. That was the beginning of the beginning—the time

when I started to feel like myself again. I had found that taking risks, being true to myself, and making decisions with good intentions can exceed even my own expectations.

DEFINING MOMENTS

That February, things couldn't have been going better for me professionally: *People* magazine named me its first Most Beautiful Woman in the World. My record was number one, my video was number one, and I was on the number-one television show in America. I felt like I was on top of the world.

In the midst of all this excitement and outpouring of appreciation and love, the bubble was burst with three simple words: "I'm not happy." Marc was in the middle of venting to me about things between us that had been

bothering him, and I was sitting there trying to figure out where he was going with it. Then he said it again: "I'm not happy. I'm here because we have a family, because we're trying to keep it together. But I'm not happy."

It was another moment where a crack appeared in yet another wall that I had built, and when the light came shining through, I immediately thought: *If you're not happy, then what am I?* I started crying. I really thought I had done everything I could to satisfy him in every way that I could—as a wife, as a partner, and as a mother to his children. But the truth was, I had never even stopped to think about whether *I* was happy.

It was like a light bulb finally turned on in my head: What sense did it make to keep suppressing my own feelings of what was missing in the relationship? How long did I need to keep trying to make someone happy who was telling me flat-out that he wasn't?

The floodgates were open, and the tears wouldn't stop. Marc tried to comfort me.

"Come on. Why are you crying so much?" he asked.

He now seemed completely fine—as if by getting it off his chest, everything was okay. To him it was some little argument, and now everything would go back to normal. I don't think he had any idea of the powerful effect those words had had on me; Pandora's box had been opened, and little did I know that, as much as I would try, there was no shutting it again.

In the time leading up to that conversation, I had been regaining my sense of confidence and self-esteem, first as a mother and then through my work. Through the kids, I had started to understand more about love and what it was to truly give love and receive it. I learned that there are certain things it's not okay to accept, and that was making me feel powerful and strong. But the thing is, in my relationship, I was still stuck in the same pattern I had been stuck in my entire life: My own happiness and sense of self-worth still depended on how happy *he* was. So when Marc stated so clearly that he wasn't happy, it broke me down completely.

For so many years I had managed to convince myself that if I worked at relationships hard enough, I could always fix everything, make things better. But now I was finally strong enough to identify not only that I couldn't, but that that wasn't the point. The point was that *my* happiness mattered too. I had reached a place where I looked at my personal life and said, *You know what? This is* not *okay.* No matter how great everything else was going in the rest of my life, this just wasn't. And I couldn't ignore it any longer.

When I woke up that morning, I never expected that such a simple conversation would lead to such an earth-shattering realization and the seismic shift it would bring upon my life.

ACT FOUR

QUÉ HICISTE

SET LIST

"Qué Hiciste"

———

"Until It Beats No More"

———

My hopes and dreams crumbled.

It was as if something had been destroyed,

something I'd worked so hard to build.

Something beautiful was breaking that I'd

once treasured.

But in its painful destruction, I found freedom.

QUÉ HICISTE

A POWERFUL MESSAGE

I'm wearing a flowing, fiery red dress while standing in front of the audience as the final notes of "If You Had My Love" play out, and I look out over everyone and say, "Sometimes love doesn't go right. And when it doesn't go right, I find that it helps to sing about it." Then the opening guitar notes of *"Qué Hiciste"* start.

> *Ayer los dos soñábamos con un mundo perfecto...*
> *(Yesterday, we were dreaming a perfect world...)*
>
> —"QUÉ HICISTE"

"*Qué Hiciste*" was the first single off *Como Ama una Mujer*—my first and only Spanish-language album. And five years later, when we were putting together the Dance Again tour, I knew I had to include the song . . . with a very important message at the end.

Whenever it feels uncomfortable to tell the truth, that's often the most important time to tell it.

This song was very hard to choreograph, because we wanted to really portray what it was about—one partner mistreating the other and the physical and emotional toll of being in an abusive relationship. Liz Imperio, the brilliant choreographer who did some of the most powerful pieces in the show—the tone setters, including both the opening and closing numbers—set about trying to make the lyrics come alive.

As I stand onstage in my red dress, a screen above me shows all kinds of explosive, fiery imagery. Lower down on the stage are two couples—one to my left and one to my right—and they're dancing, but they're also acting out the kind of abusive behavior described in the song. Liz decided that she wanted to do a beautiful fusion of hip-hop and tango. I loved it; it was a brilliant idea. It was street-hard and it was passionate, which is exactly what the emotion of the song called for.

We wanted to portray the truth about abusive relationships, but not to paint men in a negative way, even though that's how most people picture abuse. What I wanted to say is that abuse has no bias. It's not gender specific; it's just never okay. So of the two couples on the stage, one was a man being abusive to a woman and the other was a woman being abusive to a man.

You can imagine how all that went over with the audiences during our shows in certain countries where women don't necessarily have the same rights as men. When I looked out over the crowds, I could see women crying, really feeling it. And I could see the men squirming uncomfortably at the suggestion of a woman abusing a man. In some of these traditionally macho cultures, our decision to portray a woman slapping, kicking, yelling at a man was playing it a little too close to the edge—but whenever it feels uncomfortable to tell the truth, that's often the most important time to tell it.

Pulling together this song was hard on everybody, especially Liz, who got very emotional while she was choreographing it. And I understood it—it was affecting me too. But the end result was beautiful and powerful and true. As I sang, the two couples kicked and slapped and fought, but as we reached the end of the song—*"Con tus manos derrumbaste nuestra casa"* ("With your own hands, you destroyed our home")—the man and woman who had been the aggressors exited the stage, as the woman and man who had been abused turn and walk away from them. They come to meet me in the middle of the stage, right where I was standing. I turn to look at one . . . and then the other . . . and as I step forward toward the audience, they fall in line behind me and disappear. I wanted everyone to see that these people were just like me . . . even that they *could be* me.

Now I'm standing there, facing the audience all by myself, the weight of the subject matter hanging heavy in the air, the message suddenly flashes up on the screen in huge letters: *ÁMATE.* LOVE YOURSELF.

CHANGE STARTS WITHIN OURSELVES

Putting *"Qué Hiciste"* in the show, with that message, had me contemplating my past. Once again, the show was helping me face my own truth. I've never gotten a black eye or a busted lip, but I've been in relationships where I have felt abused in one way or another: mentally, emotionally, verbally. I know what it feels like for your soul to be diminished by the way your loved one is treating you . . . maybe it's a push, a shove, or a nasty word that stays with you. The scars might not be visible, but they run just as deep.

It took me years to figure out that in that kind of relationship the intensity and the conflict are really coming from two people—your partner and yourself. Because every day that you don't walk out that door, every day you accept things in your partner *and* in yourself, is a day that you're saying it's okay. Ultimately, we can never change someone else's behavior—we can only change our own.

We can never change someone else's behavior—we can only change our own.

All I could do now was figure out my own part in it. Through putting the show together, I realized that what I was working through wasn't about any one relationship, issue, or person. It was about *anything* in my life that I wasn't okay with. Anything I wanted to change. And I was getting to a point where I understood that that change had to happen within me.

Se te olvidó que era el amor lo que

importaba,

y con tus manos derrumbaste

nuestra casa

(You forgot that love was what

mattered,

and with your own hands you

destroyed our home)

—"QUÉ HICISTE"

THE END OF AN ERA

It was now May, and ever since the "I'm not happy" conversation back in March, I was living with so many unanswered questions and conflicted emotions that we hadn't addressed. Now that I look back, maybe we were both deliberately avoiding it, yet I could feel that there was a wedge growing between us. But I loved my husband, and I loved my family. I wasn't ready to give up.

The *American Idol* finale was upon us, and Randy and Steven and I were supposed to do a big performance together. It was meant to be the culmination of this great, amazing season that had rejuvenated the show—but we couldn't get Steven to agree to any of the songs. We floated a bunch of ideas out there, but for this reason or that reason, it didn't work out.

I called Simon Fuller, *Idol*'s creator and producer, and said, "We have to make this happen! It's been such a great year!" He tried, but eventually it became obvious that it just wasn't going to happen. I was disappointed, because this finale was going to be *the* show—I mean, we had a whole roster of A-list artists who were going to perform: Tony Bennett, Lady Gaga, Beyoncé, Gladys Knight . . . It was an amazing lineup of talent and we were supposed to be at the center of it, the stars of the home team. But it just wasn't in the cards.

The next day, two days before the finale, Marc and I went down to the Hollywood Walk of Fame, where Simon Fuller was getting a star. There was a ceremony, and photographers and fans were there. I love Simon and I wanted to make an appearance to support him. As soon as he saw us, he came over and drew us both into a big hug.

"Listen," he said. "Whatever you want to do on the finale, we want you to do it. We want you to be happy." I knew he wasn't pleased that the song with Steven and Randy had fallen apart. And I loved that he wanted to make it right—which was really typical of how I'd been treated by everyone at *American Idol* for the whole season.

"Maybe you guys can do something together?" he suggested.

I looked at Marc and said, "Well, do you want to do something together?"

And although I felt vulnerable in that moment, I was hopeful that it was a chance for us to reconnect and bring us close again.

"Sure," he said. "We'd have to pull it together really fast, though."

"Just let us know what you need," said Simon. "Anything at all."

"Can you fly in my band?" Marc asked. This was not a small request—Marc performed with a full seventeen-piece salsa orchestra, and most of the musicians were based in Miami and New York.

"No problem," said Simon. "We'll make it happen." And he did.

Later on, when we were riding home in the car, I suggested to Marc:

"Since your band is coming, why don't we do one of your songs . . . How about '*Aguanile*'?"

I knew that *American Idol*'s mainstream audience would be blown away when they heard Marc sing this song even though it was in Spanish. I started to envision the performance.

"I can sing it with you," I said. "I can come in on the second verse, and we can do the chorus together . . ."

But Marc disagreed. In a very matter-of-fact way, he said, "You know, this is a guy's song," and suggested that maybe he should sing and I could maybe dance.

I wasn't sure about it but I reluctantly agreed. After all, I wanted this to be good for us. I was going to put all the love and all the power I had as an entertainer and a performer into doing it.

Right away I jumped into "producer" mode. "We need to get dancers, with feathers. It all has to look really chic, with no loud colors . . ." I wanted everything to be perfect. The show was in two days, we had no time to waste. We choreographed a beautiful, sexy dance for me to do, where I came in only after Marc had already sung the first half of the song.

On the night of the finale, the show was electric. It was amazing performance after amazing performance. Finally, it was our turn: Marc sang and was blowing the roof off the place. When I came onstage and danced around Marc as he raised his eyebrows, making the crowd laugh, the audience was on ten. The last part of the song got wild, as I had even gotten Sheila E. to do a percussion solo. The moment built and built, and as the trumpets blasted the last notes of the song, I posed next to Marc, my back to the audience, my hand on his chest—giving him the final moment in the spotlight. As the crowd erupted into screams and applause, we kissed, and I reached up to wipe away the red lipstick that had come off on his lips so he wouldn't look silly.

Marc was amazing, and it turned out great. But later I realized that performance should have been the culmination of an amazing year in my life and my career and for some reason it just wasn't.

It's true that sometimes, when you're trying so hard to make a relationship work, you can sacrifice things that are important to you. And that's exactly what I was doing.

When I look back, the finale feels like the end of an era. Marc and I were magic onstage, but that was the last time we would perform together as husband and wife.

ONE LAST TRY

The night after the finale, Marc and I were scheduled to fly with the kids to the Caribbean for a vacation. I had been feeling so anxious about things between us that I wanted to take some time away from everything, to talk and hopefully reconnect.

We talked a lot on that trip, and I remember saying to him, "Marc, you and I are the glue for this family. We have to be okay, because if we're not okay, the whole thing falls apart." I told him I wanted us to spend more time with the kids, to make our family more of a priority.

As I was saying these words, all I could think was, *I hope he gets what I'm trying to say.* In fairness to Marc, I'm not sure how he remembers all this—whether he saw this vacation as a potential turning point in our marriage or not.

Sometimes, when you're trying so hard to make a relationship work, you can sacrifice things that are important to you.

We both knew something was wrong, but I'm not sure Marc looked at things as being at the crisis point that I did, or maybe he did . . . The truth was, we were talking about the same problems we always had, but what he maybe didn't understand was that even though the problems were the same, *I* was changing.

Before, I would have accepted things as they were. I'd think, *Well, that's the way it is, so I have to deal with it.* But for the first time in years, instead of taking whatever was dished out, I thought, *This doesn't feel right, and that's not good for me and it's not good for the kids.* And although Marc understood, would anything change? Or would we go right back into the same old patterns?

I got my answers the very first week we were back—the week of our seventh anniversary.

On our return home, when the day of our anniversary came up, we were trying to put everything aside and enjoy the moment, but instead what transpired was another argument.

Here's the thing about kids: They don't do what you say; they do what you do.

However, like with so many things after the babies were born, this time was different. I realized I wasn't the same person anymore and I just didn't want to be fighting anymore, I didn't want Max and Emme to think that was normal. Because here's the thing about kids: They don't do what you say; they do what you do. They watch you. If you tell them not to drink, but you drink, they will too. If you tell them not to smoke, but you smoke, you can be damn sure they're going to pick up a cigarette. So if they hear you fight or argue all the time, they are going to think that's normal as well.

I wanted to feel good about the choices I was making for myself. I wanted to be able to stand in front of them and say, "I did the right thing"—not to be some broken person who stayed in a marriage for the wrong reasons. I had fought so hard to keep things together, but you can't fit a square peg in a round hole. In this moment, I realized that no matter how hard it would be, the best thing I could do was to walk away.

There is a love like no other. A love that requires no conditions. A love that can't be explained or learned.

It's a love that gives you a greater purpose. It's a love that can set the rest of your world aside.

UNTIL IT BEATS NO MORE

WHEN YOU HAVE children, you feel love like you haven't felt before. The first time I held Emme and Max, when they were these tiny, helpless little babies, I felt such a pure feeling toward them. It wasn't traumatic, or tormented, or complicated. It was perfect and simple and true.

When I looked at my babies, I knew I never wanted to hurt them, or let anyone else hurt them. I couldn't stand the thought of it. There's a depth of feeling with my babies that surpasses anything I've ever felt before—a feeling that I'll do anything to make sure they're okay.

Romantic love is different from parental love, obviously, but it still has the same basic components. When I felt that pure love for Max and

Emme, I started to understand that something was missing from the love I had received romantically. Too often, that love felt conditional, like I had to behave a certain way, or earn it somehow, to keep it. The Bible tells us that love is patient; love is kind . . . It is not self-seeking; it is not easily angered; it doesn't keep score . . . Unfortunately, too many of the relationships I'd been in didn't quite fit that description.

It's love and I have found it, feel the beat again, stronger than before I'm gonna give you my heart, until it beats no more

—"UNTIL IT BEATS NO MORE"

LEARNING TO TAKE CARE OF MYSELF

Shortly after our Caribbean vacation, I had to fly to Europe with my mom and the kids to continue promoting "On the Floor." Our first stop was Paris. My mom could take Max and Emme out anywhere—nobody knew who they were, so nobody messed with them. They spent their days exploring the city, hanging out in parks, enjoying the scenery. Paris has really lovely parks—it's one of my favorite things about the city. So, one day when the only thing on my schedule was a performance in the evening, I said to Emme and Max, "Okay, Mommy's coming with you to play in the park today!"

My mom and I packed some snacks in a bag, and we got ready to take the kids out.

"Do you want security to come with you?" Benny asked.

"No," I said. "I don't want a bunch of people—I just want to go out with Mom and the kids."

"I don't think that's a good idea," he said. "You're going to get mobbed."

I didn't want to have to take some big entourage to go to the park. Couldn't we just go and enjoy ourselves? I wanted to believe that no one would notice we were there, or if they did, that maybe they'd recognize that we just wanted to have a nice day with the kids and give us some space. But Benny wasn't having that, so I relented and had one of our security guys come with us.

We got to the park, and the kids were really excited when they saw there was a carousel. Mom and I put them on the ride, and they laughed and shouted as they went around—they were having so much fun, and it was like a balm to my soul to see my babies so happy. But as soon as we started to relax and have fun, a bunch of paparazzi appeared out of nowhere.

We tried to ignore the pack of men circling us and clicking their cameras, though it was pretty much impossible. Still, we tried to get on with our day, and when Emme and Max saw a little booth selling toys and candy, we walked over to have a look. I told them, "Okay, you can each pick one toy." Max picked a water gun. And when Emme saw what Max had chosen, she decided she wanted one too. So we filled them up

with water, and the kids started squirting each other and running around, laughing.

The photographers kept snapping away, and they kept getting closer and closer. The paparazzi in Paris aren't the most polite or respectful. I didn't like how close they were getting especially because I had the kids with me. So I said to my mom, "Hey, I dare you to wet those guys with a water gun."

She looked at me with her eyebrows raised. "You want me to squirt them?" she asked. "Because I'll do it!"

"Ah, never mind," I said. "You won't do it. I know you won't," I added, knowing, of course, that saying that was the one sure way to get her to do it.

"Give me that!" she said, and snatched a water pistol out of my hand, charging those photographers like a mama bear on a rampage. She'd had knee surgery a few weeks earlier, so she was still limping; but she took off after those guys, shooting water right at their cameras. The paparazzi seemed terrified of the crazy lady with the water pistol, and they all started to scatter, yelling and cursing in French. But my mom kept on limp-running at everyone, spraying water left and right.

I doubled over, laughing harder than I had in months. The one thing I love about my mom is that she makes me laugh like nobody else—it's like we're connected at the funny bone or something. Whenever I'm having a hard time, I want her there, because she says and does things that always make me feel better. And this was a much-needed break from all of the intense emotions I'd been dealing with during that time.

We're like any mom and daughter in that we have our ups and downs—times where we're super loving and times when we fight like crazy. But when I'm feeling down or vulnerable or alone, the one thing I know is that I want my mom there. I know she'll do anything to make sure I'm okay; she'll hug me, make jokes, and even sleep in my bed with me if I'm lonely. Whenever I need her, she's there. I hope that one day Max and Emme can say that about me with certainty. I will do anything and everything in my power to make it so.

Mom chased after those photographers that day because she always has my back, no matter what. Because there's something about a mother's love for her kids that transcends everything.

There's something about a mother's love for her kids that transcends everything.

During that time, the strength I got from being a mom carried me through one of the most difficult periods of my life. In planning the show, I felt that "Until It Beats No More" could be a key performance depicting a pivotal chapter in my story. I really wanted the audience to see, to understand that that kind of love—the love I feel for my children—is what I consider to be the purest love of all and the impact that it had on me.

At the very end of *"Qué Hiciste,"* the words *"Ámate"* and "Love Yourself" had flashed up onto the screen. And as the piano played the opening chords to "Until It Beats No More," I would say to the crowd: "There's all different types of love . . . but then there's real, true love. And in this life, I can honestly say, I have felt true love." And then a giant photo of Max and Emme filled the screen.

I was down for the count, feeling
like I've come to the end
Nothing really mattered, nothing
left for me to mend . . .

—"UNTIL IT BEATS NO MORE"

Throughout the whole song, photos and videos of Max and Emme, many of them taken by my dear friend Ana, flashed up on the screen— a collage of so many beautiful moments we've had together. I've never been one to parade my kids in front of audiences, but I felt really strongly about this part of the show. I wanted to show people the love that had changed me. The love that had shown me that life was to be celebrated, not just endured. My babies' love saved me, and I wanted to share that with the audience too.

Every time we did this song, the audience went crazy for it. One of the things that was so fantastic about the tour was that we had all kinds of people there—from dads and moms with their eight-year-old kids, to teenagers and girls in their twenties and thirties, to middle-aged couples, to grandparents. It was a family affair, seven to seventy. And all of them responded to this part of the show, which was all about family.

There were some shows where, because of local permits and noise ordinances, we had to cut a few songs to finish in our allotted time. Once or twice, I suggested maybe we could cut "Until It Beats No More." We already had two other ballads, and I figured people would prefer the more upbeat songs. But everybody—Benny, the band, the dancers, the crew—

all said, "No way!" People felt it was the most emotional part of the entire show. In many ways, it was the heart of the show—the whole reason I was doing it. And so it stayed in . . . every time.

I'm alive, I can breathe, I can feel,
    I believe
And there ain't no doubt about it,
    there ain't no doubt about it . . .
I'm in love.

—"UNTIL IT BEATS NO MORE"

SHARING COMFORT

In the middle of the tour, I had a very special moment with Max. I brought Emme and Max on the whole tour, as I couldn't stand the thought of us being separated for five months. Fortunately, the kids are great travelers, so we didn't have any problems—although there were some very long days and nights on the road.

One night, really late, we were flying into Turkey for the next show. Everybody on the plane was asleep, passed out. But Max was awake, and he was sitting on my lap, asking me the kind of questions that a four-year-old asks: *Will you always be my mommy? When are we going to see Daddy again? Will we always be together?*

I hugged him tight and whispered, "Listen. There's only one thing you need to know. Me, you, and Emme are always going to be together, no matter what, okay? No matter what."

Max looked up at me with his big brown eyes and said, "Okay." As if that was all he needed. I pulled the blanket up around his shoulders, and he relaxed into my arms. I'd never felt happier than in that moment, because I knew it was true.

ACT FIVE

LET'S GET LOUD

SET LIST

Video transition: "Baby I Love U!"

———

"Let's Get Loud"

———

"Papi"

———

"On the Floor"

———

I am grateful for the tough experiences in my life. They taught me some of my most valuable lessons. But I can't let the negative experiences haunt my memory and fuel regret.

It's time to extract the good from the bad and leave the rest behind.

I'm taking all the positives with me and I'm forging ahead.

BABY I LOVE U!
(VIDEO TRANSITION)

AT THIS POINT in the show, there was what we call a video transition. We use these to do quick changes, but they can be so beautiful if done right and can really enhance the message of the show. Again, Parris Goebel choreographed it. It was based on a piece she had choreographed to Etta James, which I'd fallen in love with; the reason I'd hired her, actually. I asked her to do something similar to "Baby I Love U!," a song I had written many years before for my *This Is Me . . . Then* album. She thought it was a great idea. We wanted to show the blossoming of a new kind of romantic love. It was a beautiful, emotive piece, two people sitting side by side on a bench—together but independent of each other—meeting and discovering one another. It was loving but it wasn't needy; it was sweet and strong at the same time.

Creating this show and going through my songs and my life in this way was like holding up a mirror to myself. At this point in the show we had now established how people see me—Big Hollywood—how I see myself—the Bronx section—who I am as an artist and my message about love, and how motherhood had changed my entire perspective on love and how it wasn't what I thought it was. In fact, I was seeing romantic love in a whole new way. I still hadn't found the key to unlock the secret, but I was getting closer. I was in transition and this was the perfect transition piece, a perfect breather before the big finale.

. . .

Boy I never thought I could feel the
way I felt when I felt the way you
were feeling me, baby.

—"BABY I LOVE U!"

It was time to own up to myself.

Was I living the life I was supposed to live?

Were my relationships good for me?

Did I truly know myself?

TURNING POINT

ACCEPTING HELP

In looking back at the crazy ride I'd been on with my past relationships, it was hard not to recognize that there was something I needed to examine. During my trip to promote "On the Floor" in Europe, between performances and interviews, I was desperately trying to figure things out. I called my friend Leah, I needed to talk. With everything that was happening . . . I told her I'd never felt so low in my life. She asked why.

"I feel like I'm doing things and accepting things I don't want to," I said. "Like, this is not how I want my life to be. I feel sick to my stomach." No matter how bad things had gotten in the past, this was a level of anxiety I had never dealt with before. I didn't know how to handle it.

"This is great!" Leah exclaimed.

Well, that was not the response I expected.

"What's that supposed to mean?" I asked her.

"You're hitting rock bottom," she said. "You know, Jennifer, you have to hit bottom before you can make a change, and it's finally happening."

I didn't say anything. Was she right? Was that what I was experiencing?

"Do you want help?" she asked me.

"Yes," I said. "I do." I had to find some way through all this, and I didn't know how to do it alone. I had to find the strength to make a change, but I didn't have that strength in me, and I didn't know where I could get it. And that was a very frightening, disorienting place to be. I felt helpless, and I felt scared.

Leah helped me hire a therapist, and during that period, while I worked really hard promoting "On the Floor," which was fast becoming the biggest-selling single of my career, I was working even harder behind the scenes—discussing, analyzing, doing exercises, everything I needed to do to understand the turns my life had taken.

I'm usually a pretty quick study, and hot off the realization that a change was necessary, I started recognizing my own patterns. One of the most important realizations I had was that the problems I was having with Marc weren't about him. They weren't about anyone else—they were about me. And there were *a lot* of problems. One, I discovered I had low self-esteem, which I had never really pictured myself as having. Two, I worked on learning what integrity meant, which would cause a massive change—but we'll get back to that later. And three, the biggest lightbulb that went off during those two weeks was that I realized I wasn't recognizing the value of my own love.

In analyzing, step by step, relationships that went as far back as high school, I noticed I had never stopped to consider just how special *my* love was. I never stopped to look at myself and say, *You know what? You're honest, you're generous, you're loving, and you're loyal . . . You deserve a love that is as pure and special and good as the one you are giving.* My love has value. I HAVE VALUE.

Hold on, back up. I have value? My love has value?

WOW.

Sometimes, especially as women, we don't feel comfortable giving ourselves that credit. We're selfless in the best ways. But that can be dangerous too. You need to feel comfortable with affirming the greatness of who you are as a partner, a wife, a mother, a person. You are great. What you have to offer is great. When you give your time, your love, your respect, you deserve respect in return. You deserve comfort, you deserve honesty, and you deserve to feel safe. That's what relationships are supposed to be about—a place where you feel good, right?

When you give your time, your love, your respect, you deserve respect in return. You deserve comfort, you deserve honesty, and you deserve to feel safe.

Okay, so now I'm thinking, keep the diamond rings, the Bentleys, the doves, the trips to Europe . . . Keep all of it! I can buy all those things myself. Give me your time, your honesty, your respect, kindness, patience, fidelity. Give me comfort when things are tough . . . Being me, being famous, doesn't mean I don't need those things like any other girl. It didn't matter if my partners were famous either, it was always the same scenario. I gave off the air of being self-sufficient and instead of expressing and demanding the right kind of love for myself, I always wanted to appear like I was fine, in fact, I thought I was fine—and so did they. But it wasn't true. Just because you're a strong girl doesn't mean you don't need to be loved and cared for like anybody else. And it doesn't matter where you sit in this world, poor or rich, famous or not, we all need to be loved in the right way. That's what matters. In discovering my own value, that's what I was finally realizing I deserved.

I remember a time when I was filming a movie and I had finished a really good take when I started experiencing some anxiety. I couldn't quite understand why I was feeling that way until later, when my acting coach, who was on the set with me, was able to quickly notice and diagnose the problem: "You're afraid of your own greatness," she said. At the time, I didn't know what the hell she was talking about, but now, thinking back, I understand what she meant. I had never really owned that feeling. I had never truly believed I was great at acting, or anything else for that matter. I never thought of myself in that way, I wasn't even aware enough to consider it. I never stopped to give myself credit, to say, "Jen, you're awesome; you're doing amazing." It never even occurred to me. I was always working and striving and going and running. I mean I knew I was doing okay. I knew I was a good person. But *great?* I was just trying to be as good as I could be.

Marianne Williamson has a wonderful quote that says:

> *Our deepest fear is not that we are inadequate. Our deepest fear is that we are powerful beyond measure. It is our light, not our darkness, that most frightens us . . . [But] as we let our own light shine, we unconsciously give other people the permission to do the same.*

I was finally recognizing a really unhealthy pattern that had entrapped me for so many years. I was always looking for the other person to tell me I was great so I could feel good about myself. I lived for that. I wanted their appreciation. Even worse, if they didn't give it to me, I tried even harder to prove to them that I was worthy. I would keep trying to fix things and make them better, searching for that validation. I always thought the reason it wasn't working had to be because *I* was doing something wrong. So no matter how I was treated, or what the other person did in our relationship, all I cared about was getting his approval. In fact, that would oftentimes become the glue that kept these relationships together.

Ultimately, the love I wasn't giving myself, I was trying to get from others.

Ultimately, the love
I wasn't giving myself,
I was trying to get from
others.

I was so concentrated on doing everything in my power to make the other person happy, to make the other person love me, to make them believe that I was great because, deep down, I didn't really believe that I *was*.

But *why?*

I'm no psychologist, but I think much of it can be traced back to my upbringing. As the middle child, I was always trying to be perfect at everything I did in order to get some attention. I ran track and I did gymnastics and I won all these trophies and medals because I wanted my parents' recognition—and everyone else's, for that matter—I wanted them to think I was special in some way, to think that I was awesome! I always tried to be the best-hearted, nicest, most well-behaved kid. So when everyone would compliment me, in my mind, it *had* to mean that I was doing pretty well. The feeling wasn't coming from inside of me; it was coming from other people.

This thought process became a part of who I was. I would automatically feel better if someone else told me I was doing well. Having my sense of self-worth depend on someone else's validation ended up working to the detriment of my relationships.

On the flip side, that same flaw turned out to be a very positive driving force in my career. It is what fueled that overachieving quality that I had in every other aspect of my life. I am always striving for perfection and aiming for the top. But in an emotional relationship, it's a double-edged sword because the value and acceptance that can make you feel your best can also make you feel your worst when it's being manipulated or it's simply not there.

In realizing this, I understood that there was an imbalance and I needed to work on believing in myself, believing in my own greatness in order to choose the right person and make the right decisions for myself. The middle child in me was coming full circle. While I used to feel like I had to run faster than everybody, be more perfect than everybody while looking for everyone's approval, I was now finally understanding that my value didn't lie in the medals I won. Maybe just being me was enough to be loved. I wasn't giving myself any credit.

Now I knew that I had to.

Because you can't expect to be treated great if you don't first believe that you *are* great.

*Baby I need you, need you, I gotta
have you
I gotta have you baby, can't be
without you*

—"BABY I LOVE U!"

FACING REALITY

It's in my DNA to never give up, to fight to make things work and hang in there until they do. I had stayed in just about every relationship for too long, knowing somewhere deep down that I should have walked away a long time ago. This had happened so many times, over and over, in ways that were so similar. How had I not seen it before? I don't know—but now that I did see it, I knew I was never going to miss it again.

The first step in any recovery is recognizing the problem, right, folks? On this trip, I finally saw it clearly, for the first time.

On the last day of the promo trip to Europe, we were in London. I had a photo shoot in the morning before heading to the airport. As soon as the shoot was over, the reality of going back home hit me. I felt different. I went back to my room in the hotel and lay down on the bed, sobbing uncontrollably. I couldn't hold the feelings in any longer. I cried and cried. It was like an emotional flushing, like I was purging all that pain and disappointment from my system, making room for something new. Something stronger.

It was one of those gray, rainy days that are so common in London, and in the car on the way to the airport, I remember looking out the window and thinking life was gloomy, wishing I didn't have to deal with it, hoping there was a way out of the situation I was in. I was dreading going back home. Deep down inside, the fighter in me still wanted

Because you can't expect to be treated great if you don't first believe that you *are* great.

to make things work, make things better, but the reality was that I knew things could never, ever be the same.

Over the course of the previous weeks, even the previous months, little by little I had been building up my self-esteem and my self-confidence. I'd never even known I had a problem there. And one of the most important things I worked on while in Europe was finally understanding and really learning the definition of integrity.

Integrity is your own gauge of what is right for you.

Integrity is not a stand-alone concept, as we often make it out to be. *You* decide what it means to you. If you think that being talked to in a bad way is not acceptable and you allow it to happen, then you are compromising your own integrity. In other words, it's like a betrayal of yourself. And now that I was aware of that, I couldn't allow certain things to continue any longer. I would be compromising my own integrity. If I didn't take care of myself, who would?

A few days after I got back home, I was out there in the desert for that L'Oréal photo shoot, and my brain finally accepted what my heart already knew. I had changed. It wasn't about anybody else; it was about me. I knew my relationships would never be the same again.

I asked my mom if she could stay longer. "I need you," I said. "Marc and I are going to get a divorce." She knew something was up because Marc hadn't been home since I got back from Europe. She said she would, and the next day I asked Marc, who was staying at a friend's house, to come over so we could settle things.

We sat down together, and I said, "This is not working. You know it's not working. We're not living like a family, and I don't see how things are going to change." He agreed, and I continued. "Neither of us is happy, and the kids are wondering what is going on. I think we should move on with our lives."

As painful as it was, Marc seemed to know that what I was saying was true. Deep down, I still wanted him to put up a fight for our family. I wanted him to say, "No, I'm not going to let this happen."

I held my breath.

But instead, he said, "Okay." And then he added, "I want you to know, I'm always here for you if you ever need anything at all."

I burst into tears.

The only other thing I remember is that when he got up to leave, he gave me a hug. He walked out as I turned away and faced the window, but I could still see his reflection on the glass. He had stopped at the door. He stood there a moment, and then he made some kind of joke. I turned back around to acknowledge him, but I couldn't laugh—I was overwhelmed by the moment, too sad and too overcome to join in. Right then I saw Marc's whole face change, because he knew the one thing he could always do was make me laugh.

On July 15, 2011, we made the public announcement that we were going to divorce. Hardest. Day. Ever.

LETTING GO

The days following our announcement were agonizing. I knew I'd done the right thing, but it still felt very sad, our marriage had failed. And as Marc himself had pointed out, there was nothing I hated more than a failure. I was glad to have my mom there so the house wouldn't feel empty, but it still felt lonely waking up in bed alone every morning. I mourned the loss of this dream I'd had since I was young. I longed for a beautiful family and a loving husband to grow old with. I had come so close to it that to let it go now was traumatic.

As I continued to struggle with the fallout, I began to think something was still missing. Yes, I had done the therapy, made important realizations, and taken steps to do the right thing for myself and my kids. But that wasn't enough. There was something else I was seeking, something else I had to learn.

I took out some of my old books—ones that had helped me in times of need before. At first I was looking for things to help me get through the next hour, the next day . . . And then I decided to reread one of my favorite inspirational books, *You Can Heal Your Life* by Louise Hay. It's all about how you can make your own reality and your own destiny by the power of your own positive thoughts. I had always found that message—that you have the power to change how you feel, to make your own life better—really comforting, so I started reading it again.

In those weeks right after the split, I was scheduled to shoot the movie

What to Expect When You're Expecting, and I wasn't sure how I was going to get through it. Work can be great for taking your mind off of things, but I was still struggling so much. I didn't know if I'd be able to focus. But the schedule was the schedule, so I had no choice but to try and do the best I could.

There are a lot of early-morning call times when you shoot a movie. I found myself driving out to work at six a.m. each day, usually after a restless night of little sleep and feeling really depressed. There were days when I'd walk into hair and makeup, and Mary would start doing my face, just as she always did, and I'd say, "Ugh, I feel funny." I'd feel like I had something caught in my throat, or something making my chest feel tight. I'd wonder whether maybe I was getting sick, but then, suddenly, the tears would start coming—again—and I would understand that it was all those emotions forcing themselves out.

Emotional pain is such a strange feeling. You can forget you're in it—or try to, anyway—and then it sneaks up and finds its way to the surface. I felt sorry for Mary during that movie, because she was constantly using ice to reduce the swelling around my eyes. And both she and Lorenzo, who did my hair, were very sweet, always telling me, "This is normal. You will get through it." They'd let me cry for a while as they did their jobs, and then I'd finally go shoot whatever scene I had to do.

I brought my books with me to the set sometimes, and every once in a while, Mary and Lorenzo and I would read affirmations together. I ended up thinking, *I wish I could have Louise Hay here with me, to show me how to deal with all this.* It was a silly thought, coming from a desperate place. But when I told my longtime executive assistant, my great friend and confidante Debbi, how I felt, she said, "Well, why don't we call her? Maybe she'll come out to the house."

I looked at Debbi like she'd lost her mind.

"What?" I said. "Have her come here?"

And Debbi said, "Yeah. Let's call her and see. The worst that could happen is she says no!" Debbi called her, and to my great surprise, Louise Hay said, sure, she'd love to come over.

Wow . . . okay . . . Louise Hay was coming over!

A REALIZATION

On the covers of her books, Louise Hay looks young and energetic, but when she arrived at my house, I was surprised to see that she was in a wheelchair. She's in her mideighties now, but although she's not as physically spry as she used to be, she still has an amazing energy about her. She kind of sized me up for a minute, and then she got right to the point, as people of a certain age, clarity, and wisdom tend to do. (I love that. No time to waste, gotta run. I love being around people like that.)

"Why am I here, Jennifer?" she asked.

"I don't know," I said truthfully. "I just . . . Your books have always helped me through the years . . . and now I'm going through a divorce . . ." I felt a little tongue-tied, not sure how to explain why I'd asked her to come all the way to LA from her home near San Diego. "I just . . . I don't know what to do."

"I thought that's what it was," she said, and looked at me intently. "Tell me a little bit about what's going on."

I started talking about what had happened and how I felt about it.

"Well, you don't seem angry," she said.

I thought about it for a second and said, "No, I'm not angry. I'm sad."

"When a marriage falls apart, people tend to feel angry," she said. "So, that's great that you're not. Now, tell me more about what you're feeling."

So, I did. I talked about my previous relationships and how I wanted things to be right for the kids . . . I kind of laid it all out there, holding nothing back. And when I was done, she spoke again.

"You're a dancer, right?" she asked. "When you're learning a dance, if you mess up a step, you don't beat yourself up over that step, or get angry or hate yourself for it, do you?"

I shook my head.

"You just keep going and you do it again," she said. "Well, that's what you've got to do in this situation as well. You haven't gotten things right yet, but you just have to keep going with the dance. And don't beat yourself up along the way."

As soon as she said it, I realized how much I actually had been beating myself up—I'd been upset and disappointed with myself for having been through three failed marriages and for having dragged the kids into this one. When I couldn't make it work, I blamed myself.

"Fear, guilt, and blame are useless and destructive," she said. "What happened has happened. Just keep doing better and eventually you'll get the steps right."

She couldn't have said it more clearly: *Dance again!*

But it was what she said next that finally unlocked things for me.

"You know, when I first started doing my work, I would listen to people describe their problems, and then I'd try to figure out how to fix those problems," she said. "Sometimes it would work, and sometimes it wouldn't. Some people were going through rough divorces. Some people had eating disorders. Some people were drug addicts, et cetera, et cetera. So many different problems. And I was always trying to figure out the solution for each particular one."

She looked at me and smiled. "But I finally figured out that it didn't really matter what all these different issues were. There was the same basic problem at the root of them all. If I could teach people to *love* themselves, then they would wind up fixing their problems on their own."

The minute she said it, something clicked. Whenever I'd heard the phrase "loving myself" before, I'd never really gotten it. I felt like I was already doing it. I would think, *Of course I love myself! I like who I am. I work hard.* It was just a phrase to me, not something that I really knew how to do.

What was loving yourself, anyway? Nobody teaches us what that means, but now I've discovered that it's the key to life—because it's the key to loving someone else and allowing others to love you. And without that love inside, we are lost and empty shells. More practically, you have to take care of yourself, your body, your mind, take care of your soul—be your own keeper. You can give, and love, and do all kinds of things to make a relationship perfect, but if you don't think that you're great, if you don't love yourself, you'll be treated in a way that is less than you deserve. You have to make good decisions for yourself, treat yourself well. Lie down and read a book you love, or sit outside on a swing, or eat healthy—whatever it is that helps you feel good. And that includes not letting people treat you in any way that you don't want to be treated. Because when you love yourself, you don't let that happen. *That's* loving yourself.

Big. Fat. Epiphany.

You have to take care of yourself, your body, your mind, take care of your soul—be your own keeper.

Now that I got it—now that the switch had flipped on—I got excited. This was, really, the biggest epiphany I'd ever had.

"Yes . . . yes," I said. "That's so important! And you know what? We don't learn that when we're young, not from our parents, or in school, or anywhere." And I went straight into Producer mode: "Louise, we should do a kids' program, or maybe a TV show, like a Barney type of thing—but not Barney because he's corny—but something like that. Where some character sings about loving yourself . . . or . . . whatever! Do you want to work together on this? We could make something great happen! We could teach the whole world how to love themselves!"

Louise smiled and said, "Okay, Jennifer, slow down. Before you can teach anybody else, first you need to learn how to do it yourself."

I smiled back. She was right.

In the weeks that followed, I worked really hard at internalizing what I had learned. Every night, I'd take a hot bath and listen to a CD of affirmations and think about the ones that Louise had given me. Then, when I'd go to bed, I'd take it there and listen to it until I fell asleep. Over and over I would say, "I love you Jennifer, I really really love you. You are worthy of love, this whole situation is easier than I thought it would be. Me and my babies live a happy, healthy, joyful life full of love." Somewhere deep inside, I started to believe that tomorrow would be easier than today and that things would keep getting better. And eventually, they did.

I wasn't just realizing but feeling myself fill up with love and appreciation for myself. I was getting through this all on my own, and the love I was feeling inside me, I didn't need to get that from anyone else. *This changes everything,* I thought. My own happiness doesn't depend on anyone but me. Holy crap, oh my God. All that stuff you hear about love is true! Everything you need is inside of you. Love and happiness come from within. It wasn't just words anymore. I could feel it. I felt peace for the first time in a long time. There was nothing to search for or hope for in anyone else. I am complete all by myself. All on my own, I have all the love that I need.

I'm okay. Holy shit; I was doing the work and the work was working!!!

Week by week, month by month, I felt stronger and happier.

When Louise visited, I had still been crying a lot, but a few weeks later, I noticed one day that I hadn't cried yet. I looked at a clock, and it was almost four in the afternoon. It felt like a victory.

Such a strong feeling
There comes a time in everyone's
   life
When you know that everyone
   around you knows
That everything has changed,
   you're not the same
It's a new day.

—"BABY I LOVE U!"

I remember having a conversation with my sister Lynda several months earlier.

"Jen," she said, "you've always been everybody else's keeper. You've taken care of me. You've taken care of Mom and Dad and the kids . . . but when are you going to take care of yourself? When are you going to be your own keeper?"

At the time, in the midst of all the confusion, I told her, "I don't know." But all these weeks later, I finally had an answer: Now and forever.

I had truly found myself and was rejoicing in this new and tentative self-love. My loved ones surged around me, bringing strength and hope with every hug and kind word. I was healing and learning to accept their gracious support on this new adventurous and joy-filled journey.

LET'S GET LOUD

REMEMBERING HOW TO LIVE

The giant neon sign hovering above the stage says CLUB BABALÚ, and the dancers are dressed for a night out at a classic Cuban nightclub from the forties. The men are dressed in tight black suits with ruffled sleeves, white tuxedo shirts, and sparkling fuchsia cummerbunds. The women are wearing black long-sleeved backless sparkly leotards and spiked heels and are wrapped in pink ostrich feathers. The very beginning of the show was all about black-and-white, classic Big Hollywood . . . but now it's time for the colorful, loud, electrifying Latin finale.

I rise up through the stage floor, dressed in a black suit, white shirt, and pink scarf, with a fedora perched on my head . . . because I'm not a dancing girl at this club, oh no. I'm the bandleader. I'm Ricky Ricardo, I'm Xavier Cugat—I'm the one who's going to be leading this show, and I start it out with a solo on the conga. Then it's *"Uno! Dos! Tres! Cuatro!"* and the opening notes of "Let's Get Loud" kick in. It's time to celebrate life. And the whole place comes to its feet, jumping up and down, dancing, and singing at the top of their lungs.

It's party time.

*Let the music make
you free, be what
you wanna be
Make no excuses,
you gotta do it,
you gotta do it
your way*

—"LET'S GET LOUD"

The "Let's Get Loud" part of the show was all about shouting to the world that life is to

be lived! Being sad, being regretful, that's living in the past. We are here, right now, and we are going to live it up.

In the months after the breakup, I'd found myself wondering, *Where did I go for all those years?* Where was the girl who loved dancing, and didn't think so much, who allowed herself to enjoy the journey—to enjoy the steps? I had gotten lost in the pursuit of the perfect relationship and the perfect life, and as a result I hadn't really been enjoying life. Getting back in touch with that side of myself—the dancer in me—while we were doing the show, was the way to rediscover the power of my true self.

And that meant getting back in touch with my roots. I am Puerto Rican, I am Latina, and yes, I do represent. So I knew I wanted to end the Dance Again show with a big Latin blowout. It's the music of my upbringing, of my family. And at my core it's who I am.

That was the idea behind this final section, and when I started looking at my Latin-flavored hits, they all fit perfectly: "Let's Get Loud," "Papi," "On the Floor"—all songs that would get people on their feet. High-energy dance hits infused with Latin flavor. It was funny to me how perfectly the songs I wanted to do fit into each section of the show. The truth is, they all expressed who I am, or who I've been at certain times, so maybe it's not so surprising after all. Liz Imperio was doing the choreography for the "Let's Get Loud" section, and I told her, "I want it to be really exotic, really sexy. And I want it to be *big.*" I've always loved musicals—I think my mom showed me every musical known to humankind when I was growing up—and I loved the spectacle of it all. I wanted this section to be red and pink and vibrant and loud, and I even added a salsa dance break on the end of "Let's Get Loud." I wanted the audience to feel like they were suddenly in this amazing club in Havana, in the forties or fifties, with all the showgirls and all the rhythms of that era.

But I also wanted a little twist . . . It's always the girls in the sexy costumes, doing the dances for the guys, right? Well, I wanted the guys to be the eye candy in *my* Club Babalú. We had eight amazing male dancers, every one with a shaved head and a six-pack to match, and during this section, they all stripped their shirts off and threw them into the audience. They were so hot, and our female dancers were so hot, that no matter who you are or what you like, there was something up on that stage for you.

The funny thing was, two of our guys felt a little uncomfortable with this part—not because they didn't want to be shirtless and sexy, but because they hadn't really danced salsa before. They were both incredible dancers, but Latin dance is a little different, and they were nervous about it. So Liz came to the rescue, putting trumpets in their hands for "Let's Get Loud," so at least they didn't have to worry about what to do with their hands. They just had to do the basic salsa step and look amazing, which was no trouble.

That's the beauty of having a great choreographer when you're designing a show like this—Liz understood the strengths and limitations of all the dancers, and she worked around them to make sure the performances were perfect. By the end of the song, I wanted everybody to have caught the spirit—like some kind of Cuban revival, with everybody flailing around, dancing their asses off. Liz made that happen, and it was so good that the audience caught the spirit too. The whole thing was just madness—of the best kind.

THE ROOTS AND THE BRANCHES

In that crazy year leading up to the tour, my birthday was nine days after we announced our divorce. It was a particularly tough time, because while I was married we always made big deals out of each other's birthdays—and now, for the first time in seven years, I'd be facing mine alone.

I tried to act strong, like everything was fine, but inside I was struggling. It felt strange to plan a party during this time, so I didn't. I decided to go to Miami, the place I like to go whenever I'm feeling down. I'm a sun baby, I was born in July, and Miami is so sunny and warm and it makes me feel safe and happy, like being wrapped in a warm towel fresh out of the dryer. I had shot one of my first movies there—*Blood and Wine*, with Jack Nicholson—and I remember back then loving the city so much and thinking, *One day I'm going to live here, in a house by the water.* Ever since then, Miami has held a special place in my heart.

I flew down with Max and Emme, thinking I'd hang out with Ana and maybe go out on a boat ride for my birthday. Something low-key, befitting my mood at the time. I knew I was doing the right thing—this was a positive step for me, a belated acknowledgment that I deserved better. But it was still such a sad, confusing time in my life. Divorce is never easy, even if it's the right thing to do, and I felt really off-kilter.

So, I got down to Miami, and we rented a boat to take out for the day. But when we got to the marina . . . a whole group of my friends

and family were there to surprise me! My mom, my sister Lynda, my cousins Tiana and Darcy, Tania, Benny, Mary and Lorenzo, my friend Shawn B., et cetera, et cetera—it was all the people I'm closest to, and they had come here to show me support when I most needed it. I felt overwhelmed—so touched and happy, and I was excited to celebrate with all these people who cared about me.

And oh, did we celebrate. We spent the whole day on that boat—nothing but water and sunshine, good food and good drinks, and of course, great music and dancing. We blasted the music so loud that they could probably hear it all the way to Cuba, and we danced on the deck until the sun started to set. I danced with everybody, including Max and Emme—there's a great video somebody shot with their phone of me twirling Emme around in the air, both of us smiling and laughing.

I had thought this day was going to be a sad one, but instead it felt like a true new beginning. Being in Miami, with all my friends, dancing around on the beautiful, sparkling ocean helped me to truly believe that things were going to be okay. No matter what else happened, I had my friends, my family, my kids . . . I hadn't figured everything out yet and still had a long road ahead, but I was going to be alright.

We were all out on the deck, watching the sun beginning to set, when somebody brought out the birthday cake. Everyone sang, and after I blew out the candles, Benny raised his glass. Time for a Benny toast! He talked about how this day marked a turning point for me and that he and all the rest of my friends would be here to help me along the way.

It was a beautiful toast—as they always are—and when I went to hug Benny, I fell into his arms, burying my head in his shoulder. Benny just held me, whispering in my ear that I was going to be okay. All I could do was nod my head.

And then, in one beautiful moment, everyone came together and put their arms around Benny and me, and we all stood in the middle of the deck in a giant hug. It was like I could feel the roots and branches of my support system right there, protecting me and making me feel safe. All these people were here for me right now, and they had always been here for me. And I knew they always would be—that nothing too terrible could ever happen to me as long as I had them in my life.

*Turn the music up to hear that
sound, let's get loud, let's get
loud
Ain't nobody gotta tell ya, what you
gotta do*

The next day, just before Max and Emme and I were heading to the airport to return to LA, Ana came over to say good-bye. She had brought me something.

Ana likes to buy me books—loving self-help books to help me re-member to take care of myself. (In fact, she was the one who gave me my first Louise Hay book.) She handed me one and said, "I bought you this book on meditation. You have a lot of emotions going on in your life right now, and this will help you learn how to move through them." And then she handed me something else: two little ceramic angels.

"This one is Max, and this one is Emme," she said. "When you're working, put them where you can see them, and remember you have two little angels in your life." I took them from her and nodded.

She had one other thing to tell me. "Pray for Marc," she said, "and teach the kids to pray for Marc. We need to pray for everybody, and you all need to heal."

Ana and I were sitting cross-legged on the bed, and I took her hands in mine, our eyes both filled with emotion, and I thought, *This is the beauty of friendship.* Your friends mourn your losses with you, because they experi-ence them too. The truth is, no matter how lonely you might feel, you're never going through anything alone. Just as Benny would say in his toast that following Christmas, you can choose your family. Everyone who's a part of that family goes through your trials and difficulties with you.

Your friends mourn your losses with you, because they experience them too. The truth is, no matter how lonely you might feel, you're never going through anything alone.

And if you're lucky, as I am, those friends will always be ready and willing to throw you a dance party to remind you of that.

REALIGNING MY DREAMS

One of the hardest things about getting divorced is learning to let go of the dream. Because being in a marriage is all about planning the future, about hoping to spend your life with someone and trying to make that work. My dream had been to have this family forever, to grow old together and watch as our kids grew up and had children of their own. It was a beautiful dream, and it was so hard to let go of it when the time came. You end up thinking, *What do I do now?*

Funnily enough, Nancy Meyers gave me an answer. She's the writer and director of the movie *Something's Gotta Give*, starring Diane Keaton. The main character, Erica Barry, is a single woman in her fifties, with a beautiful home in the Hamptons and a grown daughter. Mom and daughter have a wonderful, close relationship, and even though she's single, Erica Barry seems to have a fantastic life.

I must have watched that movie ten times after the split. I'd be sitting there in my own nice house, dreaming about buying a nice house like Erica Barry's in the Hamptons and creating my own *Something's Gotta Give* dream life. Max and Emme would grow up to be amazing adults, and they'd come visit me, and I would end up being the kind of woman who's absolutely fine with sleeping in the middle of the bed all by myself. Thank God for Nancy Meyers, because that vision helped me get through some really tough nights.

Nancy Meyers helped me envision my dream life, but another woman helped me get through those tough weeks in real life: my mom.

My mother dropped everything and came to stay with me after everything happened. She was always there when I needed her, and the one thing I could count on was that she would always find a way to make me laugh. She's not as good at serious conversation, or the more intimate parts of a relationship, and that sometimes drives me crazy, but she will make you laugh until you pee your pants. In that way, she and Marc are a lot alike.

Mom was still staying with us at the house, helping out with Max and

Emme, when I had to fly to the Ukraine to do a show shortly after the divorce. With all the upheaval going on, and the long flights and quick turnaround, I decided it was better to leave the kids at home. I was going to be gone for only a couple of days, and I knew that doing such a long, fast trip would turn their systems upside down.

I asked my mom if she could help take care of the kids while I was gone. And right away, she said, "I don't want you to go by yourself. I'll come with you! Let Tiana take care of the babies." I frowned, and she said, "Come on . . . I've never been to the Ukraine! I want to go! I'm coming with you."

I remembered how nice it was to have her with me in Paris, when she expressed her maternal love by ambushing the paparazzi with a water gun, so I said, "Okay, Ma. Let's go together." And two days later, we were on a long flight to the Ukraine—my mom, me, Benny, and Benny's assistant.

Benny and I were sitting together in the back of the plane, talking about everything that had gone on in the last few weeks. I was still trying to sort things out from the divorce—from finances, to our home, to the kids, to all the projects that we had been working on together. Everything was so complicated, I was glad to have the long flight and a relaxed moment with Benny to talk it all through.

We were deep in our conversation when my mom suddenly limped down the aisle to our seats and said, "Jen, I feel funny."

"What's the matter?" I asked. She looked pale and kind of sweaty.

"I don't feel good," she said. "I think I'm gonna pass out." And then she did—plop! She fell right over in the aisle of the plane.

"Oh my God!" I shrieked. "Ma! Ma!" I turned to the front of the plane and said, "What happened? Did she take something?"

The assistant said, "She took a sleeping pill . . ." And of course, my mom was also still taking pain medications for her knees, having had a knee replacement not that long ago. The combination had knocked her out.

The flight crew brought an oxygen mask and tried to strap it on her face as she lay there, disoriented. I said, "Ma! What are you doing? You're supposed to be taking care of *me!*" She didn't respond, and her eyelids started fluttering. I leaned down closer to her face and said, "I swear to God, if you die right now, I will *kill you*. Do you hear me?"

And I started nervously laughing, convincing myself that everything would be fine because what else was I going to do? It was either laugh or completely fall apart.

The flight crew was discussing whether we'd need to make an emergency landing, but once my mother heard me threaten to kill her, she did exactly what I'd hoped: She started laughing.

"I'm sorry, baby," she said, still half in a stupor, chuckling weakly under her oxygen mask. We looked at each other and I shook my head. She ended up being okay, although she did have to get hooked up to an IV at a hospital after we landed. I had to tease her about being such a tremendous "help" to me on the trip. But the truth is, she was. Even when she was passing out and getting hooked up to IVs, I was so happy to have my mom with me, supporting me and keeping me laughing.

When I returned to the second season of *American Idol*, I was really happy to be back to my work family after such a difficult summer.

It was September when we started filming the auditions, and I can't remember which was our first city, but I do remember seeing Randy and Steven and Ryan and Nigel for the first time that day. We always had little sit-down planning sessions before doing the actual auditions— there was usually a big table, and food and coffee, and everyone would settle in and talk about that day's shooting.

I walked in and took a seat, and all the guys sat down. Everyone knew about the divorce by this time, of course, and right away they all started asking me, "How are you?" and "Are you doing okay?" I told them I was, and then somebody asked, "What happened? None of us expected this!"

It was true. Marc and I were great at masking the problems we'd had over the years and putting our best foot forward. I thought for a second, and then I said, "You know, it was a long time coming. We tried really hard to make it work." I didn't want to get into a whole lot of detail, but I tried to explain a little bit about what had happened.

And Steven in particular seemed to understand. I knew he had so much regret over his own divorce from his wife of many years, because whenever he'd speak about it, he'd get teary-eyed right away. He took my hand and squeezed it, and we didn't even have to say anything. Just looking into each other's eyes conveyed everything.

Then, as I looked around the table, each one of them was looking at me with such sweet concern.

"Marc was just my guy, you know?" I said, my voice cracking a little. "I thought he was my guy."

Nobody said a word, until Nigel finally said, in his lovely British accent, "Okay, darling. We don't have to talk about this anymore." He knew it was getting too deep, and we had to get in front of the cameras soon.

"Let's pull ourselves together," he said, clapping his hands. "We're ready to go, here." He left the table and went to the set, and we all followed him out.

I walked out onto the set like everything was fine, and we started doing the auditions—a normal day, as usual. I'm listening, laughing, being pensive, being emotional, just doing my thing, living the moment. Then I looked over to the side, where Nigel was sitting. Our eyes met, and he mouthed, "I love you." I mouthed back, "I love you too." He understood, and he appreciated the fact that I was there, doing my job, despite what I was going through.

That's always how it was on *American Idol*, because *these* were my guys too, the people who supported and appreciated and respected me. Doing that show felt like wrapping myself in a security blanket . . .

Which is, in some strange way, why it became so important for me to walk away from the show. In fact, doing that ended up feeling every bit as important as walking away from my marriage.

RISING TO THE CHALLENGE

I had just started the Dance Again tour when Benny told me I had to make a decision about doing a third season of *American Idol*.

Over the past year, I had undertaken two of the scariest things I'd ever done. The first was finally deciding to move on. The second was deciding to do the world tour. I had been so afraid of it all—afraid I would fail, afraid people would criticize me . . . I'd gone back and forth so many times with Benny when he was starting to make all the arrangements, because I couldn't convince myself it was worth all the risk.

And then I realized something. I realized that if I didn't believe in myself, nobody else would either. What was I so afraid of? What was the worst that could happen? Whatever it was, it couldn't be worse than simply being too scared to do anything at all. If I didn't do this tour, I'd probably regret it for the rest of my life. So I finally decided to make the leap, to choose to believe in myself.

We had been on the tour for only about a week when Benny said, "We have to talk about *Idol*." My second season had gone as well as my first one, and the producers wanted me to come back. It was so tempting, for all the same reasons I'd done it to begin with.

And yet . . . all the events of the past year had changed me in ways I was only beginning to understand. When you make hard decisions, when you follow your heart to places that terrify you, it's no longer possible to simply choose the easy path. My life was in transition, and it was a transition that I had chosen. I had to follow it through to the end.

So, when Benny asked me, "What do you want to do? What would make you happy?" I realized there was only one answer I could give. I loved being on *Idol*, but it was time to move on. It didn't make sense for me to spend a third year in a row sitting on a panel, judging other singers, especially if the main reason I was doing it was for the security of it.

The irony is, being on *American Idol* for two seasons was the very thing that gave me the strength to realize I needed to get back to doing the other things that I do. It was the spark that led me to value myself more, to respect myself as a person and as an artist. And now I had to use that newfound self-respect to put down the security blanket. I knew it was the right thing to do, but it was still so very hard.

We were on the tour, somewhere in Canada, when I called Ryan Seacrest to give him the news.

"Hey," I said, "I'm so grateful to all of you for everything, but I've decided I'm not coming back next year."

I was really emotional, and so was Ryan. He told me he wished I would stay, and I told him a part of me really wanted to, but right then I just couldn't.

"I feel like we're breaking up," he said.

"I do too," I told him. "This show has meant so much to me. Thank you, and I'm sorry." I barely managed to hang up the phone before I was overcome by emotion.

Benny put his arm around me and asked gently, "Are you okay?"

I said, "Yeah. It's just so hard to do." In some way, walking away from *Idol* felt tied to walking away from Marc—it felt like the final act in a play, the inevitable, emotional conclusion.

Benny understood.

"Being on the show gave you the strength to walk away from other things," he said. "It's like you're walking away from a whole period of your life."

Just a year earlier, it would have been really easy for me to decide to stay in both situations—my marriage and the show. There were plenty of reasons to stick with both, and the idea of leaving either one of them filled me with fear. Now I had confronted that fear head-on. I hadn't

When you make hard decisions, when you follow your heart to places that terrify you, it's no longer possible to simply choose the easy path.

allowed it to dominate my life and my decisions. As painful as it was at that moment, I knew that my life would ultimately be better for it, both personally and as an artist. And you know what they say, set something free, and if it comes back to you . . .

And the amazing thing was, it happened as I was beginning the Dance Again tour—the tour whose whole message was to live again, and love again, and *dance again*, to take chances and put yourself out there.

In choosing to leave *Idol*, I was putting that into action, really living it. Once the initial shock wore off, it felt like a weight had lifted off me. Like I'd been underwater, running out of breath, and finally dropped enough weight to float to the top . . . only to find that glorious moment when all of a sudden your head pokes through the water's surface, and there's air, and sunshine, and you can breathe again.

So, when I stood up on the stage in city after city and said to people, "You've got to love yourself," I really felt it. Because I was finally living it.

THE PERFECT ENDING

"Turn up the lights!" I'd shout right after the end of "Let's Get Loud." "Let me get a look at everybody!" And no matter what city or country we were in, I loved to look out and see so many girls in the audience.

"I see a lot of beautiful ladies out here tonight!" I'd say. "All my girls came out! Let me hear you!" I'd point the microphone out to the audience, and the women would all scream.

In a lot of the places we performed, women don't have as much of a voice as the men do, so this part of the show was always one of my favorites. It was like a competition. The women would yell and stomp their feet, and then I'd call out, "Where my papis at?" And the men would let out a roar.

Back and forth I'd go—"Where my ladies . . . ? Papis, let me hear you!"—and I loved to hear how the ladies would let loose. The women were always louder than the men, and in their screams and shouts, I felt like they were shouting, *We're here. We're not afraid. And you are going to hear us!* Sometimes I'd go back and forth five or six times, talking to everybody, inviting them to let loose.

Then I'd say, "We did a lot of songs for the ladies tonight . . . And, ladies, even though you obviously won, let's do one song for the papis. But keep a close eye, because there's something extra special in here for you." And we'd launch into the song "Papi"—which seems like it would be for the guys, but really, it was for the ladies. At one point, the male dancers would take off their J.Lo tanks and throw them into the audience for the women to take home. A memento, from me to my girls, to remind them that we were in control that night. And then, for our last song of the night, an explosive finale— the biggest hit of them all: "On the Floor."

*Dance the night away
Live your life and
stay young on
the floor!*

—"ON THE FLOOR"

I started "On the Floor" singing a cappella in Spanish, a slowed-down version of the chorus: *"Llorando se fue y me dejó sola sin su amor . . ."* ("He left crying and

left me alone without his love . . .") It was kind of a callback to where this journey had all started, both literally and figuratively. Every night it reminded me of what I'd been through and how far I'd come during the last year. I had been so afraid to embark on this journey, yet here I was at the end of it, feeling stronger than ever. My voice had grown, I had grown. I had changed so much. I wasn't singing the way I did before—the fear was gone and I was better than I was when I started. I had found my voice; I had found myself. The journey was complete. I'd repeat the chorus line again, one more time, holding the last note as long as I could, echoing my newfound strength. The audience would yell in appreciation, and as soon as the first chords of "On the Floor" rang through the arena, all hell broke loose. We were all about to rip the roof off the place. A throne rose up from the floor, a moment for me to sit down (thank God—after two hours I had earned it!) while Pitbull's verse ripped through the speakers. Two of the dancers would bring me a black silk robe with a beautiful feathered boa collar as I walked down the stairs while singing the first verse of the song. By the time we hit the chorus again, all twenty thousand people were jumping up and down in unison, fists in the air, singing:

Laaa lalalalalala lalalalala la la laaaa
Tonight we gonna be it on the floor . . .

It was the perfect ending, a euphoric climax, a moment of true abandon where we were celebrating life to its fullest.

The crowd loved it. The show is over . . . but there's one more song to come, the encore, the song that brought the whole thing together . . .

ENCORE

My dream as an artist is to share my

experiences in a way that will touch people.

"Dance Again" allowed me to create

something beautiful from the ashes of

the pain.

This is my moment.

DANCE AGAIN

SEARCHING FOR THAT ONE LOVE

In October of 2011, just three months after Marc and I announced our separation, I was scheduled to do a one-hour show at the Mohegan Sun Casino in Connecticut, six months before the Dance Again tour even started. I didn't have anything pulled together—we had to create the show from scratch.

We were going to have to throw it together quickly. And once we had the whole thing figured out, there was still room for one more song. I decided I wanted to put in one of my new songs from the album I'd just released, *LOVE?*, one that people might not know that well, but that spoke to the situation everyone was still talking about—my divorce. I hadn't made very many appearances since our official announcement, so people were naturally curious: *How is she doing? Is she going to talk about it? Is she okay?* I decided I'd give them something to satisfy that curiosity.

The song, "One Love," from an album aptly titled *LOVE?*, was another song I had written—this time with the help of Anesha and Antea, two writers who contributed to the album greatly—it was about a woman's search for that one true love. When we wrote it, we made the verses very autobiographical, describing in detail some of my past relationships. It's a really intimate, personal song, and as we started working up the choreography, I decided, *What the hell. I might as well just lay it all out there.* So we worked up a staging of the song that would walk everybody through my life and past loves, one by one.

Is there one love, only once in a lifetime?
It's so hard to find, the perfect one to call mine.

—"ONE LOVE"

But the night of the show, I got cold feet.

"This is too much," I told Benny. "I feel too exposed putting all this out there right now. It's too soon." I told him I wanted to pull the song.

"Listen," he said. "You're the one who's always saying that being an artist is about baring your soul, about being introspective and making yourself vulnerable. So, if you feel vulnerable right now, then I guess we're doing it right."

"I know. I know," I said. "But I'm really uncomfortable doing this right now, okay?" Benny was firm, using all of my own arguments against me. He loved the number, and he loved the statement it was making. And as much as I didn't want to admit it, I knew he was right. All those beautiful words about what it means to be an artist were only words unless I followed through with them. So I did.

And this is how it all played out . . .

I was standing onstage, dressed in a white gown, and I sang the first verse of "One Love":

Took a shot with the bad boy from the block
Picked my love right from the start,
Mister Wrong, he plays his part.

To my right on the stage stood a man wearing sunglasses and a gray suit and a woman dressed in that famous green Versace gown—Puffy and me. Their images were projected on a giant screen above my head, so nobody could miss the point. I kept singing:

Back to the beginning, now round two,
Try my luck with something new
We danced until we said "I do,"
My luck is bad, no more us, two, no me and you

That was Cris and me, of course. To my left on the stage was a man with a shaved head, kneeling to propose to a woman. She had her hair in braids and was wearing a J.Lo shirt from the "Love Don't Cost a Thing" video, in which we'd famously danced together. Now the next verse:

It's take three, could there be a part for me?
Came and swept me off my feet
Went nowhere but kept the ring,
Once again, I'm lonely

And to my right, a tall, handsome actor with a woman wearing a mint-green dress, her hair pulled into a bun—just as I'd dressed to go to the Oscars with Ben in 2003 . . . And then finally:

Number four, you sang to me but I'm not sure
So worn out but loved you so
Made me wanna try once more
and I couldn't say no

To my left, a dashing man singing into a microphone while I danced around him in a short, sparkling dress—just as Marc and I had danced on the finale of *American Idol* only a few months earlier.

Is there one love?
Somebody that complements me
And makes me wanna never leave
Made just right for me
Is there one love, one love, one love, one love . . . ?

As the song came to an end, I had seen my four great love affairs flash before my eyes. I looked over at the dancers playing Marc and me, and the whole thing felt so surreal. I got stuck there looking at that image.

As I sang the final line—"Is there one love?"—I turned and faced the audience and I just stood there, still, looking out over them for a moment that seemed like an eternity . . . They were feeling everything I was feeling, and I was feeling them right back. We were sharing a real moment. It's one of those things that happens onstage when you truly connect with your audience.

I couldn't think of what to say. There were no words. All I could do was lift my hands and shrug my shoulders. At that moment, the place erupted. Their cheers transitioned from applause for the performance to a warm embrace of love. I could hear people screaming, "We love you, Jennifer!" and "Keep your head up!" and "It's gonna be okay!" I felt so emotional. Tears started welling up in my eyes. It was like they were telling me they understood that I was a girl, like any other girl, just trying to get it right. In that moment, I thought, *It doesn't matter what the tabloids print, or the picture other people want to paint—I can come onstage and show people who I really am.* It was a beautiful, powerful moment for me. For us.

Months later, when I was planning the world tour, I realized I could never perform that song again. It was a one-time thing, perfect for that moment in time, but it would never be as special as it was that night. That song was all about my past. It was over now, and I was looking toward the future.

BUILDING MYSELF BACK UP

In those first few months after the split, I certainly wasn't looking for anyone new—how could I? I had to get my shit together, to figure out why I'd been repeating the same pattern over and over every time I was with someone. I was sad, and hurt, and confused. But a part of me also felt stronger, like I had finally taken a step toward respecting myself. I lay low for a while, but when I started up again with projects that brought me back into the orbit of music and dancing, and we were in full pre-production of the tour, I began spending more time with Beau.

Throughout that whole fall and into the New Year, as we got more and more into the heart of the show, I started moving past the hurt, and believing there could be something after that, believing that I could *dance again.*

From the very beginning, whenever I would stumble, whenever I was unsure, Beau would say, "You got this. You can do it." But he took it even further, telling me, "You don't need me. You don't need Benny. You don't need your mom. You don't need Marc. You are always going to be fine."

And I realized that before, my relationships were always tinged with fear: *Is this going to last forever? Will he want to stay with me? Is this going to work?* But now, I don't worry about the future. My idea of forever has been shattered. Now, I just want to be happy. I want to be in the moment and learn to be happy.

LOVING THE JOURNEY

About three weeks before the end of the tour, all of us were feeling it. We still loved doing the show, but all of the travel, the hotel rooms, the time zone changes, and being away from home took its toll on everyone. Doing such a high-energy show, night after night after night, meant that everyone was feeling tired and rundown. And I knew that when the

tour was finally finished, I wouldn't miss all that packing and unpacking, bundling the kids up to get on buses and planes at three a.m., waking up and wondering what country we were in . . .

But then, one night in the dressing room just before I was supposed to go onstage, a thought popped into my head: *You are about to make so many people happy tonight.* Where had that thought come from? I had no idea, but it made my heart swell with joy. And I realized what I *was* going to miss when the tour was over.

When I decided to take on this tour, I was still at a low point from the divorce. I felt like things in my life had gone wrong, and doing this show was going to be my effort to make something go right—by using the experiences I'd had and choosing to learn from those difficult times rather than running from them.

My one job was to go out there and make people happy every night, to help them jump and dance and sing along, to make their lives a little bit better. What a blessing! For years, I had been afraid to do a big tour like this one, but by the end of it, I felt like it had healed me. My original intention had been to share this message with the world, this thing that I had learned about loving yourself and overcoming adversity. I wanted to put it out there: *You will live. You will love. You will dance again. Ámate. Love Yourself.* I never expected it, but I wound up living my own affirmation, every single night. Life is kind of awesome that way; when you put things out there, they end up coming back to you.

ON THE MEND

Doing all those shows, and being embraced by the crowds, was a cathartic process that helped me heal. Benny could see it too, so one day toward the end of the tour he made a suggestion that he knew I wouldn't have been able to consider even just a few weeks earlier.

The last days of the tour were upon us, we had been talking about what we could do to make the final performance, in Puerto Rico, really special. By that point, we would have done more than seventy-five shows, and we both wanted to go out with a bang.

"What do you think about having Marc come perform a song with you at that final show?" he asked.

For a moment, I was speechless. My mind flew in two different directions: The professional side of me knew that doing a performance with Marc, who's a legend in Puerto Rico, would be amazing. People would go crazy, especially if we kept it a secret until his actual appearance.

I thought about that, thought about whether doing this would be like giving the spotlight to Marc on that *American Idol* finale, letting him have a moment that might have been mine. Was I falling into the same old pattern that I had spent months pulling myself out of? Would inviting him to sing with me be a step backward?

By now I had learned to listen to myself. And when I got quiet and listened to my heart, I really didn't believe it was. Asking Marc to join me onstage wasn't about reverting to old habits. It was about showing the world—and proving to myself—that not only did we make it through the pain, but we came out the other side even stronger. We came out of it in a healthy way, and we were moving on as friends and as parents to our children. I really believed that making this offer to Marc was about moving forward, not backward.

Life is kind of awesome that way. When you put things out there, they end up coming back to you.

I still had to call Marc. He's pretty picky about when he chooses to go onstage, and this performance would have that extra layer of prurient interest for people, so there was a good chance that he would immediately say no.

I called him up, and at first we talked about the kids for a little while. Then I said, "Listen, Benny had this idea for the last show of the tour . . ." I told him the last two shows were going to be in Puerto Rico, right before Christmas, and of course we needed to figure out when he was going to see the kids around Christmastime anyway . . . so . . . "I was thinking . . . it could be really beautiful . . . if . . . you came down . . . and did 'No Me Ames' with me in those last shows." Then we could figure out the holidays.

He didn't say anything, so I went on. "I think it would be amazing for the audience . . . I think they would love to see us together, knowing what we've been through, and that it could be a great message to everybody that we still support each other." I told him it had been a difficult time for me, and I knew it wasn't easy on him either, but that this could be good closure for us.

"Mm-hmm . . . okay," he said, and I could practically hear the wheels turning.

"We wouldn't announce that you were coming—it would be kind of a surprise for everybody," I said. "We'll make it really great."

He said, "Well, it's not a 'no,' but give me a day or two to think about it." I thought that was pretty reasonable, considering everything.

A few days later, he called back . . . It was a "Yes!" He would do it.

The day before the show, Marc flew down to Puerto Rico to rehearse with us. Marc had recorded *"No Me Ames"* with me on my first record, so we didn't need much rehearsal for the singing; we just needed to figure out the staging.

When Marc walked into the stage area, Max and Emme went running up to him, excited to see him. And a lot of the dancers made a point of coming to watch the sound check too, because they were big fans of Marc.

At one point, I looked over and saw Marc sitting on the floor with the kids. They were so happy to be with him; they were climbing all over him. At that moment, the band started playing the opening notes of *"No Me Ames,"* which was one of the first things Marc and I had ever done together, so we have a lot of memories associated with that song. The whole scene was so surreal. When those notes started floating out over the stage, I looked down at him, and he looked up at me and laughed.

"How the hell did all this happen?" he asked me. And I knew what he meant. He meant everything—all the crazy twists and turns our lives had taken since we first sang that song together. How did we end up recording this song all those years ago, and how did we not get together then? And then how did we wind up getting married years later, having kids, and then divorcing . . . and now how was he sitting here with our kids, looking up at me as this song played again? It was this lovely, bittersweet lifetime of moments, all summed up in that one question.

"I don't know," I said. And we laughed. But it was a heavy moment, and I think everyone there that day could feel it. The fact that we'd been through so much, I had invited him to come, and he was there to support me—it was a moment filled with every kind of emotion. Just like life is.

On the night of the show, I did something I rarely do—I decided to speak in Spanish to the crowd. I'm Puerto Rican, but I grew up in New York, so although I speak Spanish pretty well, it's not my first language. But I wanted to do it, to speak the language of the crowd, because I wanted this night to be magical for everyone:

"Estas son nuestras últimas actuaciones de the Dance Again tour. *Esta gira ha sido un viaje increíble de música y amor. Y ha sido un honor y un placer terminarla aquí en Puerto Rico, donde hice mi primer concierto hace once años. Y como todos los grandes viajes de amor y música, incluso cuando se terminan, la música sigue..."* ("These are our last performances of the Dance Again tour. This tour has been an amazing journey of music and love, and it has been an honor and a pleasure to end it here in Puerto Rico, where I did my first concert eleven years ago. And like all great journeys of love and music, even when the journey ends, the music goes on . . .")

With that, the band played the first few notes of *"No Me Ames,"* and I turned to face the back of the stage, where Marc was rising up slowly through the floor. As soon as his face was visible, the place erupted—the crowd went absolutely insane, everyone was screaming so much that the band actually had to stop playing. It was pandemonium, people yelling and crying and clapping . . . Marc took a little bow. And then we started the song.

Dime por qué lloras
De felicidad
Y por qué te ahogas,
Por la soledad
(Tell me why are you crying?
Because I'm happy
And why are you so choked up?
Because I'm lonely)

Singing with Marc felt like a perfect, beautiful closure to that part of my life. Things might not have worked out the way I had planned, but I was so proud of where we had come, especially after all that heartache. It was the perfect ending to those two years of turmoil and confusion and sadness, and ultimately, recovery. It was the perfect start to the rest of my life.

When we finished the song and ran offstage together, I had my arm around him, and as soon as we were in the back, he exclaimed, "That's what the fuck I'm *talking* about!" He was as happy and excited as I was. He gave me a big hug and said, "If you ever need anything . . ." His voice trailed off. We looked into each other's eyes.

"I know," I said.

He squeezed my hand, we both smiled . . . and off he went.

But the show wasn't over, of course. It was time for me to do a quick change and get out there, because now it was my time to *dance again*.

I WILL ALWAYS REMEMBER

The arena is completely dark. Suddenly, on the big screen above the stage, I appear like a black butterfly, with a black mask and the wind blowing through my hair. Quotes from different interviews I've done over the past year appear on the screen: *I still believe in love. It's still my biggest dream. You have to truly love yourself to be able to love another.* It's the encore of the show—the final song, the final message. I look out over the audience and say the words, "Always remember . . . You will live. You will love. You will *dance again*."

When I first thought of this mantra, I was doing the video for "Dance Again." I wanted people to really understand what the song meant to me. It was a declaration that I needed so much in my life at that moment, and that I know other people need in difficult moments of their own lives. I tried to think of the perfect line to put at the front of the video, a simple phrase that could help you get through any difficult moment . . . And then it came to me: I wasn't going to die, I was going to survive. Things were going to get better, I just had to hold on. I was going to live, I was going to love, and I was going to dance again . . . I just had to remember that.

And so that's what it was. After all, that was the theme that started it all. This is where we always wanted to end up. On that note.

My face disappears from the screen, replaced by the words: "*Ámate.* Love yourself."

The spotlight goes up on the stage, and I start to sing.

Only got just one life this I've learned, who cares what they're gonna say?
I wanna dance . . . and love . . . and dance . . . again.

Yes, I still believe in the fairy tale, but I want love in the right way. I want the kind of love that's truly possible only when you love yourself first. This is my favorite moment in the whole show—the moment when we get to the "Dance Again" chorus, where everybody in the whole place jumps up and down, waving their arms, singing at the top of their lungs, "I want to dance . . . and love . . . and dance . . . again!" At that moment, the elation in the arena is like a revival. It is transcendent.

In every city, every night we performed, this was the moment that made me feel it was all worth it. All the pain, all the regret, all the uncertainty had led to this, to sharing myself with all of these screaming, jumping, sweaty fans, all of us shouting this one big affirmation together.

And then, of course, when the dance break comes, the lights go low and it's art imitating life imitating art again . . . I'm dancing a sexy, fresh, totally revitalizing dance that reminds me, every time I do it, that life goes on and why I love to dance so much.

It's the perfect way to end the show—with a new beginning.

Love...
For me is a journey,
its not a destination.

I remain an
eternal optimist
about love

I want the fairytale,
its still my biggest dream.

You
must love yourself
to truly love another.

Always remember . . .

You will live. You will love.

You will *dance again*.

CONCLUSION

TRUE LOVE

IT WOULD BE easy to look back on those years leading up to the divorce and think, *Oh, this is a really sad story. That was so hard.* But I don't feel that way anymore. Now when I look back, I feel something completely different . . . pride. For so many years, when I was in situations that were bad for me, I was afraid to leave them. Then, somehow, I finally found that little speck of love inside myself that said, "Hey, you deserve better." And I actually did something about it, as scary as that was.

I'm proud that now I can make better choices for myself and for my kids. That finally, after forty years, I was able to understand what I was doing wrong. Proud that once I got okay with the fact that being just me was enough, I actually became a better version of myself—as a person and even as a performer. At first, I felt frustrated that it had taken me so long to figure it out. But then I ran across this quote from Charlie Chaplin:

> *As I began to love myself, I freed myself of anything that is no good for me—food, people, things, situations, and everything that drew me down and away from myself. At first I called this attitude a healthy egoism. Today I know it as* love of oneself.

That quote is from April 16, 1959—the day Charlie Chaplin turned seventy. So, I guess in some ways, I'm ahead of the game, right?

And yet . . . the truth is, I'm still a work in progress. I'm still learning. When you've been doing things a certain way for your whole life, you can't suddenly behave in a different way overnight. It takes time. You have to start practicing it, and little by little you keep practicing, and eventually it becomes second nature. We all second-guess ourselves,

doubt our own instincts, and forget to love ourselves—especially women.

As women, we almost never give ourselves enough credit for what we're capable of, for what we endure and how giving we are. During the tour, I would look at all the amazing, beautiful women in the audience, and I wanted to pull them all into an embrace, to tell each one, *You're great. Trust yourself. Love yourself.* The emotion was overwhelming at times, especially in those countries where women aren't held in the same esteem as men. I wanted to open their hearts and pour the love right in.

Part of loving yourself is about forgiving yourself—which is something I've always struggled with. Being ambitious, being a perfectionist, means I've spent my life beating myself up for not being good enough, or for screwing something up. It took a long time, but I finally figured out that I wouldn't have half the instincts or insights I've had as an artist over the years if not for those screwups. It's the messy parts that make us human, so we should embrace them too —pat ourselves on the back for getting through them rather than being angry for having gotten into them in the first place. Because loving yourself is ultimately about self-acceptance, about embracing every part of who you are. And that's never just one

thing. For example, when it comes to my music, I have never been about one thing: I can make a booty-bopping record that makes you want to dance all night and I can also create an emotional heartfelt ballad that makes you contemplate life and love in all its complexity. I've always been pop, but I've been hip-hop too, I've been R&B, I've been Latin, I've been ballads . . . and I feel very comfortable in every one of those places. Why limit myself? I realize that you have to be real, you have to be as honest as you can be and not worry about judgment or criticism. I have to accept all of that and I have to love all of that because that's what being a true artist is about: knowing yourself, accepting it all, and sharing it with others. And that's what I work on every day.

Even though I still have a ways to go, my family and friends tell me they can see the difference. Benny even jokes about it with me—if I disagree with him about something, or stand up for myself, he'll say, "Okay, okay, I get it. You're loving yourself!"

He teases me, but then he has moments where he'll say, "You know, Jennifer, you're like a different person now. You make different decisions; you don't stand for the injustices anymore." And he's right. I don't. I'm quicker to stand up for myself, to push back if someone is treating me in a way I

Sometimes you have to explore the darkness to get to the light and get back to who you are.

don't like. I've always pushed back if I see someone else being mistreated, but it took me decades to figure out how to push back for myself.

But as I've been reminded, a lot of people never figure it out at all. We all know someone who's had their hopes and dreams and belief in love destroyed because they couldn't figure out how to value themselves. "You did it," Benny says. "Even though it hurt so bad while you were doing it, you still did it."

My life now might not be how I always envisioned it, but that doesn't mean it isn't great. If it weren't for this tour, this time, these kids, that marriage, I would never be where I am today, which is the best place I've ever been in my life.

I found that same girl again. Sometimes you have to explore the darkness to get to the light and get back to who you are.

That's the whole message of the Dance Again tour, of course: We can survive anything, if we just keep on going.

This road of healing and rediscovery has been a long one, and it was much more difficult than anything I've ever done. It's taken me to some real emotional lows. But the view from the other side was worth the heartache.

Like Louise taught me, I keep dancing. I may not be getting all the steps right yet, but I'm dancing my heart out. I am the woman I've always wanted to be because for the first time I can truly say that yes, I love myself. That's the key. That's the greatest love of all, the one that matters most, the one that Max and Emme taught me all about.

That's TRUE LOVE.

ACKNOWLEDGMENTS

MUCH LIKE THE year I went on tour, writing this book has been another incredible journey—one that could have never happened without the love and support of so many people who have helped me along the way.

First off, I would like to thank my family: Mommy, Daddy, Leslie, and Lynda, thank you for supporting me all these years and for being the loving family you have always been. I could have never gotten to where I am without you and I love you so much. To my cousins Tania, Darci, and Tiana; and to my Titi Rose—thank you for being there every step of the way.

Thank you to Benny Medina, my manager and friend for over fifteen years who has been my partner in every new adventure I embark on and writing this book was no exception. Your wise words and comments made every page of this book even better and I am so grateful to have you in my life.

Thanks to Raymond Garcia, my publisher, for your dedication, enthusiasm, and unfaltering belief in this book, even when I had my doubts. Writing this book has been one of the most gratifying and enlightening experiences of my life, and I would have never done it if it hadn't been for you. Thanks to Andrea Montejo for your editorial support during our "booking" sessions and for helping me cut, paste, and rewrite until it felt just right. Thanks to everyone else at Penguin who helped make this book a reality: Jennifer Schuster for your editorial direction, Kim Suarez for photo editing, Matthias for the cover photo, Pauline Neuwirth for the beautiful interior design, and Anthony Ramondo for designing the cover.

Thank you to Marc Anthony, Leah, Elaine, Loren, Ana, Kevin, and all of my close friends for reading the first drafts of this book and giving me your precious feedback and comments. Thank you to my dear friend Ana Carballosa, to whom we owe the beautiful photos that truly bring this book to life.

Thanks to my personal team: Debbi Izzard, Day Ryan, my home team in LA and NY; my team at Nuyorican Productions, JLE, and the Medina Co.; Kevin Huvane and all of my agents at CAA; my attorneys; business partners; and of course to my loving fans . . . I appreciate you all.

And last, but not least, thanks to my beautiful babies, Max and Emme, for being the light of my life, the reason for everything I do, and for being exactly who you are. Mama loves you very much.

PERMISSIONS

NEVER GONNA GIVE UP
Words and Music by MICHELLE BELL, PETER KEUSCH, and
JENNIFER LOPEZ
© 2007 120 MUSIC PUBLISHING, UNIVERSAL MUSIC CORP. and
ELLEGANZA MUSIC PUBLISHING and NUYORICAN PUBLISHING
All rights for 120 MUSIC PUBLISHING Administered by KOBALT MUSIC
PUBLISHING AMERICA, INC.
All rights for ELLEGANZA MUSIC PUBLISHING Controlled and Adminis-
tered by UNIVERSAL MUSIC CORP.
All rights for NUYORICAN PUBLISHING Administered by SONY/ATV
MUSIC PUBLISHING LLC.
All Rights Reserved.
Used by Permission of HAL LEONARD CORPORATION.

WAITING FOR TONIGHT
Written by MARIA CHRISTENSEN, MICHAEL GARVIN, PHIL TEMPLE
Published by Sweet Woo Music (SESAC), VMG Notation Songs (SESAC),
Michael Garvin Music (BMI), VMG Notation Worldwide (BMI), Soulspin
Music (ASCAP), VMG Notation Copyrights (ASCAP)
Administered by Wixen Music Publishing, Inc.
Used by Permission of Wixen Music Publishing, Inc.
© 1999

I'M INTO YOU
Words and Music by DWAYNE CARTER, TOR ERIK HERMANSEN,
MIKKEL ERIKSEN and TAIO CRUZ
© 2011 WARNER-TAMERLANE PUBLISHING CORP., YOUNG MONEY
PUBLISHING, INC.,
EMI MUSIC PUBLISHING LTD and KOBALT SONGS MUSIC
PUBLISHING
All rights on behalf of itself and YOUNG MONEY PUBLISHING INC.
Administered by WARNER-TAMERLANE PUBLISHING CORP.
All rights for EMI MUSIC PUBLISHING LTD Administered by SONY/ATV
MUSIC PUBLISHING LLC.
All rights Reserved. International Copyright Secured. Used by Permission.
Used by Permission of ALFRED MUSIC
Reprinted by Permission of HAL LEONARD CORPORATION.

GET RIGHT
Words and Music by RICHARD HARRISON, JAMES BROWN and USHER
RAYMOND
- contains a sample from "Soul Power '74" by James Brown
© 2005 DYNATONE PUBLISHING COMPANY, EMI BLACKWOOD
MUSIC INC., EMI APRIL MUSIC INC. and UR-IV MUSIC
All rights for EMI APRIL MUSIC INC., EMI BLACKWOOD MUSIC INC.,
and UR-IV MUSIC Administered by SONY/ATV MUSIC PUBLISHING LLC.
All rights for DYNATONE PUBLISHING COMPANY Controlled and
Administered by UNICHAPPELL MUSIC INC.
All Rights Reserved. International Copyright Secured. Used by Permission.
Used by Permission of ALFRED MUSIC
Reprinted by Permission of HAL LEONARD CORPORATION.

LOVE DON'T COST A THING
Words and Music by DAMON SHARPE, GREG LAWSON, GEORGETTE
FRANKLIN, JEREMY MONROE and AMILLE HARRIS
© 2001 WB MUSIC CORP., DAMON SHARPE MUSIC (ASCAP), VMG
NOTATION COPYRIGHTS (ASCAP), SWETTE YA' MUSIC, GQ ROMEO
MUSIC (BMI), VMG NOTATION WORLDWIDE (BMI), J-RATED MUSIC,
WARNER-TAMERLANE PUBLISHING CORP, EMI APRIL MUSIC INC.,
J-RATED MUSIC, ANGEL OF MUSIC and REACH MUSIC SONGS
All rights on behalf of itself and SWETTE YA' MUSIC Administered by WB
MUSIC CORP.
All rights for EMI APRIL MUSIC INC., and J-RATED MUSIC Administered
by SONY/ATV MUSIC PUBLISHING LLC.
All rights for Damon Sharpe Music (ASCAP), VMG Notation Copyrights
(ASCAP), GQ Romeo Music (BMI), VMG Notation Worldwide (BMI)
Administered by Wixen Music Publishing, Inc.

Used by Permission of Wixen Music Publishing, Inc.
All Rights Reserved. International Copyright Secured. Used by Permission.
Used by Permission of ALFRED MUSIC
Reprinted by Permission of HAL LEONARD CORPORATION.

FEELIN' SO GOOD
Words and Music by SEAN "PUFFY" COMBS, CORY ROONEY,
JENNIFER LOPEZ, JOSEPH CARTAGENA, CHRISTOPHER RIOS,
and STEVEN STANDARD
- contains elements of "Set It Off"
© 1999 EMI APRIL MUSIC INC., JUSTIN COMBS PUBLISHING
COMPANY, INC., SONY/ATV MUSIC PUBLISHING LLC, CORI TIFFANI
PUBLISHING, NUYORICAN PUBLISHING, JELLY'S JAMS LLC, JOSEPH
CARTAGENA MUSIC, LET ME SHOW YOU MUSIC, STD MUSIC
PUBLISHING and REACH MUSIC PUBLISHING, INC.
All rights on behalf of SONY/ATV MUSIC PUBLISHING LLC, EMI APRIL
MUSIC INC., JUSTIN COMBS PUBLISHING COMPANY INC., CORI
TIFFANY PUBLISHING, and NUYORICAN PUBLISHING Administered by
SONY/ATV MUSIC PUBLISHING LLC.
All Rights Reserved. International Copyright Secured. Used by Permission.
Reprinted by Permission of HAL LEONARD CORPORATION.

GOIN' IN
Words and Music by JOSEPH ANGEL, MICHAEL ANTHONY WARREN,
TRAMAR DILLARD,
DAVID JAMAHL LISTENBEE, DAVID QUINONES and COLERIDGE
GARDNER TILLMAN
© 2012 WB MUSIC CORP. (ASCAP), ROC NATION MUSIC (ASCAP),
HEAVEN UNDERGROUND MUSIC PUBLISHING (ASCAP), SWEETER
THAN HONEY MUSIC (BMI), SONY/ATV MUSIC PUBLISHING LLC
(ASCAP), GOONROCK MUSIC (ASCAP), EMI BLACKWOOD MUSIC
INC., SO GOOD IT'S RIDQULOUS MUSIC, and COLERIDGE TILLMAN
MUSIC (BMI)
All rights on behalf of Itself, ROC NATION MUSIC and
HEAVEN UNDERGROUND MUSIC PUBLISHING Administered by WB
MUSIC CORP.
All rights on behalf of SONY/ATV MUSIC PUBLISHING LLC, EMI
BLACKWOOD MUSIC INC., and SO GOOD IT'S RIDQULOUS MUSIC
Administered by SONY/ATV MUSIC PUBLISHING LLC.
All Rights Reserved. International Copyright Secured. Used by Permission.
Used by Permission of ALFRED MUSIC
Reprinted by Permission of HAL LEONARD CORPORATION.

JENNY FROM THE BLOCK
Words and Music by TROY OLIVER, ANDRE DEYO, JENNIFER LOPEZ,
JEAN CLAUDE OLIVIER, SAMUEL BARNES, JOSE FERNANDO
ARBEX MIRO, LAWRENCE PARKER, SCOTT STERLING, MICHAEL
OLIVIERE, DAVID STYLES and JASON PHILLIPS
- contains samples of "Hi Jack," "South Bronx," and
"Heaven And Hell Is On Earth"
© 2002 SONY/ATV MUSIC PUBLISHING LLC, MILK CHOCOLATE
FACTORY MUSIC, JAEDON CHRISTOPHER PUBLISHING, TUNESMITH
ADVANCEMENTS, NUYORICAN PUBLISHING, JUSTIN COMBS PUB-
LISHING, EMI APRIL MUSIC INC., PANIRO'S PUBLISHING, UNIVERSAL
MUSIC PUBLISHING – MGB SPAIN, UNIVERSAL MUSIC – Z TUNES LLC,
JACK RUSSELL MUSIC LTD and JAE'WONS PUBLISHING.
All rights on behalf SONY/ATV MUSIC PUBLISHING LLC, MILK CHOCO-
LATE FACTORY MUSIC, JAEDON CHRISTOPHER PUBLISHING, TUNE-
SMITH ADVANCEMENTS, NUYORICAN PUBLISHING, JUSTIN COMBS
PUBLISHING, EMI APRIL MUSIC INC., PANIRO'S PUBLISHING JAE'WONS
PUBLISHING Administered by SONY/ATV MUSIC PUBLISHING LLC.
All rights for UNIVERSAL MUSIC PUBLISHING – MGB SPAIN in the U.S.
and Canada Administered by UNIVERSAL MUSIC – MGB SONGS
All rights on behalf of JACK RUSSELL MUSIC LTD. in the U.S. administered
by NW COLLECTIONS.
International Copyright Secured. All Rights Reserved.
Reprinted by Permission of HAL LEONARD CORPORATION.

ABOUT THE AUTHOR

JENNIFER LOPEZ is an award-winning actress, singer, dancer, entre-
preneur, fashion designer, film producer, philanthropist, and now author. She is one of the most influential female artist-performers in
history and proud mother of the two children, Max and Emme.